SOM journal

1

Hatje Cantz Publishers

Contents

Introduction

External Criticism

An unusual invitation was sent at the end of 2000 by the partners at SOM to five individuals: the artist Jenny Holzer (New York); the architect Jesse Reiser (New York); the structural engineer Cecil Balmond (London); the architect, historian, and critic Kenneth Frampton (New York); and the architect and critic Wilfried Wang (Berlin).

The invitation asked the five whether they would be prepared to sit in judgment of some forty-six projects currently under way in the four offices of SOM: New York, Chicago, San Francisco, and London. The group was chosen not only to constitute a jury of experts in their respective fields, but also because each one of them is known to have more than a passing interest in the other's field of expertise. This fact was borne out in the subsequent discussions of individual projects: the comments were perceptive, concise, and complementary. The unusual synergy evidently present during the selection process contributed to the comprehensive and concentrated assessment within one day.

The jury's task was to select five to six schemes for the new *SOM Journal*, the first in-house journal of the work of a practice whose contents is entirely edited by outsiders, an unusual process that comes as close to an objective assessment as can be considered possible.

All five invitees agreed, a date was found, and the jury met on March 18, 2001 in the New York offices. The five invitees shared an interest in the evaluative process of one of the world's largest practices; they were curious to understand the kind of work that the practice has been pursuing in recent years. Was it going to be a dry affair, or would they be able to trace some new developments at SOM? Would it be a diplomatic job, would they have to hold back in their criticism, or would it be an open and insightful event?

The conditions for the jury were clear. There were no restrictions, encouragements, or other distractions by any member of SOM during the judging process. The five members of the jury were free in their establishment of selection criteria, and it was left up to them to include or reject any scheme. Such clarity was self-evident; without these parameters, none of the jurors would have taken part.

The forty-six projects were presented with four or five small digitized plots including a description. These were mounted on the walls of two meeting rooms. The morning was spent gaining an understanding of the schemes, and a first round of discussions as well as selections was begun. After lunch, the focusing on a dozen or so schemes took place, with a final round of selection and elimination in order to arrive at five to six schemes.

The edited transcript of the jurors' comments is included in this publication and accurately reflects the considerations and sentiments of the individual jury members. Formal voting took place to establish a minimum vote of one in the first round, followed by majority voting in the subsequent round. The last five schemes and the one research project were in fact chosen unanimously by acclamation. Now, in turn, with this publication the jury's selection is open to critique by the interested public.

SOM's invitation to a jury of experts from different

fields for the purpose of judging the current output of all of the offices across the world naturally raises questions as to why there would be an interest to undertake such a potentially fraught process. Which office has ever undertaken such a "glasnost," such an external review? In leaving the selection criteria open, what would be the outcome of such a process?

In any normal competition, the result of the selection produces winners and losers. Thus, the rejection of the one project and the inclusion of another are associated with feelings of disappointment on the one hand and pride on the other. No doubt, once the results became clear, those sentiments were indeed felt by the various participants, from team members to the different partners. No doubt, many questions were raised that had not occurred to those who had previously considered this undertaking. No doubt, the charge that the result would have been different with another group of critics would have crossed the minds of some participants, particularly in the aftermath of the announcement. However, as a process of continuing evaluation, the annual review of the most innovative projects of the practice will surely be seen by all—inside and outside the office of SOM—as an unprecedented critical discourse on architectural quality and themes. The five invited critics understood this selection process as part of the practice's interest in raising the design profile both in and outside the practice, hence the *SOM Journal*. For this reason, the often used interpretation that the long-term result could in fact be the raising of general standards might indeed hold true. The critical review in the media of this outcome as well as of this journal will give further indications of the undertaking's relevance and sincerity. Since the review process is to continue next year with the same jury, time then will tell whether it will have an impact on the architectural discourse at large and on the internal debate within SOM.

With this review procedure, SOM is moving beyond the practice of internal, imminent criticism employed at design schools, where outside critics are periodically invited to comment, but hardly to select and rarely to grade the work. The faculty at most architecture schools are still as protective of their school and their students' work as any small or large practice. Some schools even tend to invite friendly critics only, those empathetic with the direction of the school, or—put in another way—those critics who better understand the ideology and who share the concerns of the influential faction of the faculty.

In the USA, such bastions of school styles have been built across its territory, bastions which lay claim to a particular, not to say the only true, pedagogy. Within this state of affairs, new academicizations have taken root and no doubt will last as long as the respective deans remain in office. Architectural practices, in a similar way, have been strongly influenced by their partners, whether small or large in scale. In the case of large practices, a certain in-house style might have been established by the time the founding partners have retired or passed away. It is then a matter of transforming, adapting, and modernizing the practice's approach; a process that may or may not take place. A second, third, and subsequent generation takes hold and reinterprets the approach and values of previous members of the corporate practice. Who structures such a search? Who has the time, inclination, and commitment to direct such a research within a constantly stressed practice? Does this transformation not take place pragmatically, learning by doing? Is there such a moment in which more conscious reflection is expended on structuring such a *revirement*? At SOM, the partners have taken the initiative in this matter, the first result of a broader exploration that is under way being the review process by outsiders as documented by this new journal.

To our knowledge, no other publication such as this one exists. There are many vanity monographs funded by architectural firms, many with introductions by significant critics. In its history, SOM too has had its share of such publications, and recently, SOM's preparedness to allow the commentating critic to truly reflect on the quality of the work is again unparalleled. It is probably true to claim that the jurors' comments contained in the edited transcripts are on occasion incisive to the point of being painful to the authors of the schemes, while on other occasions they are commendatory. Mostly, however, the remarks are on the spot. In the future it would be interesting to include another level of criticism from the readership of the journal. In any case, the fact that such a process is taking place already expresses the lucidity of the partnership currently in charge at SOM. It is a level-headedness based on the awareness of the directions and abilities of the other offices, a self-understanding of its own strengths and weaknesses, an assuredness of the directions it can give in terms of a professional service as well as in terms of the more specific architectural discourse that gives SOM the confidence to pursue this process.

Having reached the end of the selection process, the jurors were satisfied, while different segments of SOM reacted in different ways. Given the many projects from the New York office, no doubt questions have been asked within the practice and are bound to be asked outside it. Central to the jury's consideration, however, was the notion of the contribution that a building makes to the discourse of architecture. Where are there recognizable improvements or innovations to the way that buildings transform and modernize use? How does a building synthesize operational demands with modes of awareness? Where are the realms of freedom for architecture at a time when structure, cladding, and services have all become part of the optimizing package of any development? How can the onerous demands on the smooth coordination of the various subcomponents be superceded by interests beyond these hypercritical professional services? How can long-term projects (both in terms of their gestation as well as in their life expectancy) simultaneously lead the otherwise forever evolving, fast-changing architectural discourse while also establishing fundamentally valid terms for some time to come? From these points of view, a number of projects within the office suggest a departure from the classicizing designs of the 1980s and early 1990s and a *return with a difference* to the apparently more stringent formal interests of the 1960s, the difference

resting in the inclusion of local particularities or picturesqueness within an overall sensibility of the sublime. One of the commonly perceived sources of such a compositional approach can surely be seen in the Neoplasticist paintings and architectural compositions of the 1920s as well as in the wall and windows of Le Corbusier's chapel at Ronchamp, a motif that has been much quoted and adapted, not only by the designers at SOM. It is this notion of the "both/and," where the overall form is clearly structured and understood, while internally a highly differentiated form of articulation, nevertheless strict in the observation of familial relationships, is pursued. Inspired by the task, the best of these schemes currently under development in the SOM offices involve this approach across the depth and breadth of the overall design.

Directing Architecture

Viewing the production of one of the world's largest architectural practices, it is easy to overlook the changes in the nature of the client while insisting on an almost moralistic, architectural consistency in that practice's output. The change in direction from the earliest serenely rational offices and educational institutions to the embracing of historicist compositional techniques and forms to which in-house commentators of late have referred, specifically of the period of the 1980s, has not only affected large practices such as SOM, but almost all offices active during that period. Various abridged versions of the classical orders were put through the collagist paces of purist compositions, finding respective echoes not only in the work of the former members of the New York Five (Michael Graves and Richard Meier), but obviously in much mainstream corporate practice.

Like many practices of this period, SOM fared well with the design approach of rerooting late 20th-century construction in the traditions of the city or more specifically in the formal tradition of so-called "high architecture." Urban design schemes were thus part of the new palate of commissions for large practices, coinciding with the first wave of globalized investments. The scale of such investments was unprecedented. They were able to fund the construction of entire city quarters, and the building industry was geared to their construction. These investments needed faster income and income on a guaranteed scale so as to satisfy impatient and optimizing fund managers. Sites for these city quarters had to be already well served with infrastructure or such infrastructure would have to be provided without convoluted planning approval processes.

It comes as no surprise then that the first and most visibly entrenched urban schemes in the historicist imagery were the master plans for London's Canary Wharf (realized from 1988 onwards) in the specially ear-marked enterprise zone established under the premiership of Margaret Thatcher, followed by the superstructures over Bishopsgate (1988–92) and King's Cross railway stations (1988–97, project only). These urban developments were part of London's expansion in the speculative office sector, giving rise to unusually high densities, deep plans, and rapid construction. The attitude in many of the buildings that form a part of these new urban quarters asserts a traditional order, an assertion that has as much to do with the reaction to the mistakes of conventional modernism as with a homage to the decorative role that architecture had once again to play for corporate clients.

There is no question that the direction of architecture did not only take place within the confines of the architects' practice, but that, in London, additional significant pressures were placed on the clients and thus on their architects by such organizations as conservation groups. However, it is equally fair to say that the production of much Anglo-Saxon architecture at that time was determined by a pervasive interest in architectural history. The recent monograph by Abby Bussel (Basel 2000), entitled *SOM Evolutions*, while making an editorial reference to the problematic era, cuts short the practice's history by establishing a bridge between the earliest work and the renewed interest in the reticent—or in current parlance, "cool"—tectonic and constructional rationalism. However, such a selective re-presentation of a practice's output, although no doubt creating an image of seamless continuity in some less well-versed observers, mistakes the bridge building for establishing continuity where on the contrary there is severance and ignores the power of each act in a chain able to induce reactions.

One notable aspect of SOM's design history is the search for coherence in the work. In this regard, the internal debates and team discussions have always been intense; the conceptual and intellectual consensus reached, even by team members whose previous interest was focused in other directions, is noteworthy. There is an outward representation of a collective attitude and a collective responsibility, a central quality in corporate practices, seemingly following the dictum: strength in unity. The process required to achieve that unity at SOM is complex, on certain issues cumbersome, and on others imposing. Client and contractor liaison, legal issues, office management, design team structuring, best-practice detailing and specification, external communication, and other central professional issues have been constantly developed and documented. Such concentrated knowledge alone behind the collective design work would merit analysis and would find extensive readership.

Directing architecture within a large practice requires on the one hand strict rules as well as personal involvement; on the other hand, in order for larger questions of culture, political discourse, and the more general considerations in the domain of art and design to be creatively absorbed into basic approaches to architectural design, the large practice needs to allow space for intensive internal debates that might indeed have a competitive dimension. In this connection, for instance, the extravagant manner by which overall solutions as well as components have been developed in Norman Foster's office—where a number of design groups make proposals for the same design problem and the partners in charge select one version, rejecting the others—has shown that internal debate and competition are unsubstitutable catalysts for the office's aspiration to be part of the architectural avant-garde.

The Selected Schemes: Architectural Issues at the Fore

The five schemes and the one research project selected contain issues that have been addressed in other designs submitted to the jury. That is not to relativize the process of commendation, but rather indicates that, aside from the reading of the larger architectural development, an exchange of ideas is taking place within the office.

The jury's establishment of a different award category, namely the research project, was based on the precise but fragmented work presented by a series of smaller projects that were presented together because they did not have the independent, object quality that the other submitted schemes had. These smaller elements were part of entrances, infrastructural links such as bridges or stairways. The jury felt that they were as important as the free-standing pieces in the definition of a coherent and well-designed environment. The jury was particularly impressed by the composition of steel and glass for the Jubilee Park Pavilion (London) as well as for the People Mover Station (Detroit). Here the overall statement of the relatively small buildings was seen as more consistent than the structurally and programmatically more complex San Francisco International Airport. Though the jury acknowledged the integration of structural symbolism of the open arch trusses at the airport, the more direct reading as well as the greater control over the specific dimensions in the smaller infrastructure projects swayed the decision in favor of these research projects.

The shared interest in segments of spheres can be seen in the giant glazed steel structural shell that spans the gap between the two masonry buildings at Penn Station (formerly the James A. Farley Building for the U.S. Postal Service by McKim, Mead & White, 1914), in the competition entry for Christ The Light Cathedral in Oakland, California, and even in the roofs for the grandstands at Ascot Racecourse in England or for the Algarve Football Stadium. These dominant formal gestures have the added task of not only providing quotidian shelter, but also symbolically charging the space with a monumental spirit, fragmentally referring to the Pantheon or more 20th-century industrial structures as the archetype. The complexity of movement, the specific orientation of the segmental dome, the idea of an embrace as passengers enter and leave New York City via the dramatically covered ticketing hall, the movement thrust from the basement tracks: all these moments provide more than a simple logic to the segmental dome's existence. Therefore, beyond the structural or even formal interest that the segmental dome holds, the Penn Station scheme provides the most comprehensive instantiation for the integration of such an unusual element. The jury was quite aware that the dome could easily be regarded as a conversation piece, casting into shadow all the other important and difficult design issues such as providing a clear sense of direction between the levels, offering an efficient relation between the service elements such as ticketing and the tracks, not allowing the complexities of retail aspects (deliveries, fire hazard) to gain the upper hand, or indeed allowing issues of lighting and air conditioning to weaken the clarity of the space and structure. The Penn Station design thus shows how minds can be concentrated on apparently one important formal item, thereby disciplining the nature of the other components.

Taking the theme of cladding, the degrees of transparency/opacity constructing a variegated surface of an almost mosaic-like diversity can be seen not only in its most radical form in the roof of Singapore Airport Terminal Station, but also in a more planar, but not to say less considered manner for the office tower extensions for 350 Madison Avenue and the New York Stock Exchange, as well as the skin development of the high-rise on Riverside South (Site B). This ludic aspect of the surface to an otherwise geometrically compact set of forms owes something to the already mentioned composition of windows seen in Le Corbusier's chapel at Ronchamp, while a similar, seemingly irregular structural patterning can be seen in Le Corbusier's La Tourette Monastery.

Specifically for 350 Madison, the jury was impressed by the project for a vertical addition to an existing piece of fabric, something perhaps unique to the

States (thinking of the early Bostonian example of Customs House), in contrast to the European paradigms as exemplified by Erik Gunnar Asplund's Gothenburg Law Courts extension (1913–37). Here is the chance to work within the urban tradition of spatial and formal types, while also highlighting the fact that the addition is a contemporary element that consciously marks a separation between itself and its base. The rotational and cladding aspects underline the object status, more so than for instance Christian de Portzemparc's Fifty-seventh Street LVMH tower.

These surface articulations of the SOM projects are a result of contemporary construction technology avoiding cold bridges and thereby confining the otherwise tectonically visible frames or subframes to the interstices of the overall envelope. Gordon Bunshaft's investigations focused on the continuation of Miesian *in situ* and prefabricated façade frames, into which glazing or cladding panels would be inserted, subsequently embracing not so much frames as lattices but frames resulting from nodes, so the St. Regis Museum Tower makes use of the computer's power to control complex folds and geometries, moving the theme of cladding to the realms of the tectonic and sculpture (the architectural team cites Balzac's pose with a coat thrown over his shoulder by Rodin).

Bunshaft's direction of the practice during the 1960s and 1970s spanned from the sublime reinterpretation of the idea of post and beam of antiquity (for example, see the headquarters for the Emhart Corporation in Bloomfield, Connecticut, 1963) to the repetition of a miniature order across and atop one another to form a lattice (see the Beinecke Rare Book and Manuscript Library at Yale, 1963, or the headquarters of the Banque Lambert, Brussels, 1965). There were essentially two types of junction in these schemes: planar and corner connections. Such discipline produced a coherent order; at the same time, these mostly orthogonal parallelipipeds could be sensed as monoliths, thereby once again underlining that repetition of surface elements over a certain scale and number transcends an immediate sense of order and instead establishes the megaform.

There appear to be two general types of investigations in vertical surface articulation. Firstly, by means of alternative materials creating a mosaic that is constituted by a complex algorithm, controlling, say, a second-order gradation from top to bottom of increasing transparency—a quasi graphic version of the ancient Greek formal device of *entasis* (for example, New York Stock Exchange and Riverside South Site B). Such surface articulations tend to support the primacy of the configuration; the mosaic is scaled in such a way that it is not read as a camouflage transfiguring the massing of the building. In the case of Singapore Airport Terminal Station, the louvered roof with its apparently irregular canopy has the atmosphere of dense foliage. Its overwhelming size, diffuse light, and almost infinite extension have the fundamental qualities of the sublime. Given these qualities, Terminal 3 at Changi Airport in Singapore was recognized by the jury to most comprehensively relate this type of formal investigation into the articulation of surface, boldness of architecture, and appropriateness of spatial expression.

The second type of investigating surface articulation is achieved by geometric variation (St. Regis Museum Tower), in which each rule of articulation exists in support of the "drape" of the cladding, the "fall" of the cloth, or the figurative dimension of the building's configuration. Such investigations, when carried out in relation to high-rises, recognize the narrow conceptual base for which such efforts are expended. There often are no relations between skin or indeed cladding type and interior spaces. Thus when additional spatial and organizational manipulations become possible within the building's program, albeit allied to the physiognomic concern for identifiability within an overall recognizable geometric structure, the most developed example of this can be seen not only in the design for the Informal Office for Singapore, but also in the abstract-structural conception of the Greenwich Academy with its top-lit courtyards in counterpoint to its dominant horizontal planes. Both the organizational variegation as well as the surface articulation recall the discourse of indeterminacy theorized by John Weeks (of Llewellyn-Davies, Weeks, Forestier, Bor; see the organization of the circulation system and the façade design of the Northwick Park Hospital in London, 1962–64) and by Candilis, Josic and Woods, specifically for the so-called "mat building" for the Free University in Berlin (1963–79). In turn, these designs owe a debt to Le Corbusier's monastery at La Tourette (1957), even if the former's scale of operation is larger and their spatial and organizational differentiation more elaborate.

In the Informal Office for Singapore, the programmatic interplay of low and high-rise slabs recall the flexibility of Centre Pompidou (Renzo Piano and Richard Rogers, especially the competition version of 1970). The structural system of triple-story diagonal grids is also reminiscent of Louis Kahn's Tomorrow's City Hall project for Philadelphia (1952–58). What were logistical nightmares have, with the aid of the computer, become eminently realizable projects. The Informal Office could become a synthesis of half a century's strife for the taming of inner-city sites by means of multifunctional megastructures, albeit of a kind that comes closer to the ludic positivism of earlier Archigram fantasies. If Kazuyo Seijima's Gifu Kitagata housing slab at Motosu, Japan (1994–98) is a spatial and typological interplay within tight dimensional margins, a development of Le Corbusier's Unité Marseille (1946), then the Informal Office is the next step in the lineage once begun with the Pavillon de l'Esprit Nouveau (1925).

Aldo van Eyck's Orphanage (Amsterdam, 1957–60), in which there is a concatenation of formal decisions, each at different scales but each in turn formally related to one another, could be argued to foreshadow many of the design considerations of the Kuwait Police Academy. Notions of a geometric unit as a module, of a relationship between circulation armature and the resultant constitution of space, and of a hierarchy of rooms (from the honorific to the quotidian) can be traced in parallel between seminal projects by the 1960s Team Ten members (Smithsons, Giancarlo de Carlo, Bakema, Candilis, Woods).

The basic components of the academy, the so-called "rope building" developed to recall the geometry of Kufic texts, form the courtyards. Three stories tall, they define neutral enclosures for daily routines. Set among these differently paved or lined yards are the honorific buildings, shaped like lozenges and dramatically lit at night. In the entire volumetric and constructional detailing, from the geometric control of the configuration to the shape grammar of the precast concrete panels, both repetition is achieved as well as the identity of each unit established. Light chambers as spaces of reflection, designed by James Turrell, are to provide moments of repose in the hallways. Overlaid on the entire complex is a continuity of materials such that the material of the ground planes of one courtyard covers the adjacent building. The design of the Kuwait Police Academy could thus be considered to encompass the office's comprehensive design and professional abilities on the one hand, and on the other hand underline the unusual conceptual aspirations turned into an architectural proposal for a client who probably did not initially realize that such a construct could be possible. The scale of the project, the authority of the architect defined as knowledge in design, and the client's trust in the design team have opened the view to the new.

The Responsibility of the Large Practice

The last decades of the 20th century saw fundamental changes in the nature of clients, in the scale of operations of the property market in general, in the cultural aspirations of communities as remote as Bilbao, in the complexities of construction technology, in the repercussions of professional liabilities, in the nature of construction documentation, and in the sophistication of built and written architectural discourse. There is no doubt that changing generations of responsible and influential team members in large practices have more naturally adapted to these circumstances. Without doubt, SOM as one of the leading firms of this type has undergone constant transformation not only to divest proper professional services in space planning, but to raise the stakes once again at the core of architecture's concern, that is, to transform an apparently unemotional brief into an inspiring confluence of space, light, and matter. In rising to such occasions—and by no means are these occasions either available or taken with every commission—the authority and physical size of the practice divests more than its due. The five selected schemes and the one research project as well as the related interest shown in the other projects mentioned here demonstrate that unsuspecting clients can benefit from the ambitions and skills housed in such large firms. The secret of how clients are convinced and how a firm such as SOM builds the right team at the right time in order to produce outstanding designs will of course remain as such. The architects at SOM, that much is sure, are there to write a further chapter in the practice's history.

Wilfried Wang, Berlin, June 2001

Jury Transcript

Jesse Reiser, Jenny Holzer, Kenneth Frampton,

Cecil Balmond, and Wilfried Wang

March 18, 2001

14 Wall Street, New York City

WILFRIED WANG: It would be useful to have a general discussion of your impressions following your initial view of the forty-odd entries. Perhaps you'd like to raise some of the issues that you noted. These could help us frame the selection process, since there's both a diverse range and a diverse scale of buildings, as well as diverse locations. In order to set up some criteria by which we can then make a selection, maybe a short discussion would help to identify what is uppermost in your minds. So who would like to begin?

CECIL BALMOND: From my point of view, there's a lot of potential in the buildings and the engineering. Some of the projects had an opportunity to clearly bring out the architectural hypothesis, but this opportunity was not always seized in a more holistic sense. In some of the projects we're shown an interesting text, but I couldn't find images to match the discourse,

while on the other hand, some images might be more compelling if the designer were here to talk. I'm trying to be as fair as I can. By which criteria should we judge a good design? Are they the way SOM meets their client's brief? Or are we judging the six best projects in terms of how the designs meet the views of the design community, or indeed the needs of the community at large? Those are the first thoughts crossing my mind.

KENNETH FRAMPTON: Without entering into the substance of a particular work for the time being, there is a paradoxical communication problem: on the one hand, the advantages and disadvantages of computer graphics can be strongly felt. On the other hand, seen from the communication point of view, it's hard to get at the strategy behind the designs. What was the intention? Something that could have been carried in a sentence or two, but those sentences more

often than not are missing. It's as though we've entered a conversation that is already under way.

CB: I feel the same. I sense that often the presentation does not do justice to the work. One just feels that somehow there was more earnestness and much more of a design objective in some of these projects than we are given to understand.

KF: These computer graphics completely dematerialize the buildings. I've never experienced this before with such clarity. In a number of projects, this kind of dematerialized representation is part of the design's seduction. The problem is we don't get beyond those dematerialized images until quite late in the game. The Columbus Center building is astonishing from this point of view, because it is just being built, but in terms of graphics it is still hovering like a phantom. I find that amazing.

JENNY HOLZER: I think that next year, those submitting the work should be encouraged to write a little more completely about the problems that they encountered, the charge that they were given, what they were attempting to do, and what they were able to do. It doesn't have to be more than a paragraph, but I would like a short history of the effort, and an outline of the constraints and the opportunities.

JESSE REISER: I perceive a pivotal moment in at least some of the work at SOM. I sense that, from the very strong legacy of the firm, especially the early history, there is an effort to bring back organizational and systemic interests as seen in buildings like Lever House. This hinges on some of the comments Ken made. This is a moment when the economy of construction and the knowledge of a pattern of construction in a space comes into contact with new tools: the computer and computer-linked fabrication. What is most easily modifiable under this new model would be something like a curtain wall system that one could engineer, producing a continuous variation of

panels or of solar screens. Very impressive work. I was really taken with it, but at the same time, one can see the tension between normalization of the spatial model and the activation of skins. The 200 Broadway project begins to make some connection between a new way of organizing space and the envelope. However, here one gets the inverse: the diagramming of space as a continuous flow, while the envelope remains fairly undeveloped. There are some competing tendencies which I can see coming together in the future. But generally, I was tremendously encouraged by certain projects, because in them I do see a loosening of the organizational models, and an attempt to balance new paradigms and corporate modernism.

CB: I agree, but in an office like this, the firm's structure with partners running separate agendas, there is bound to be a range of work. I guess there would be a pedigree of offices in the Lever House tradition running through, right? And I think the Museum of the Skyscraper is an attempt to evoke that. I like that. And then you get the beginning, late in the day, the current fashion run. There are a few shapers at work here. There are one or two little projects here where the shape or something more fundamental is trying to drive the form, trying to drive the organization. But they're not presented well enough to understand whether they will affect the organization in terms of people's movement or what the

building does. Nevertheless, an interesting spread. There is a seriousness of work here that is impressive. But we don't know enough. And some projects probably fell off my list because, while there was something there, the presentation wasn't convincing.

WW: Well, it strikes me that a number of these buildings are really about a design struggle, as Jesse identified. However, the people involved in these designs, from the partner to the project architects, are fully aware of what's happening outside, of course, not just in the field of architecture, but also in the field of the fine arts. We've had lots of references to the fine arts in the descriptive texts. Whether that's post-rationalization in the knowledge that there would be an artist on the panel, I don't know. So they're fully aware of the discourse that's going on, and I think the tension that Jesse has described between the normative organizational aspects of buildings such as offices of this kind inevitably have to address and the attempt to create something different, to make a mark, is most noticeable when the forms are being manipulated,

the surfaces are being made interesting and relatively irregular. Sometimes this is done with a straightforward interest in just making a difference, which seems alright. What one is now looking for is a link to issues of ecology, energy management, and issues of new organizational structures, as one can see for instance in Foster's Commerzbank high-rise in Frankfurt.

KF: Some of these projects are not in America; they're in Europe. Some of them are floating in Ken Yeang's territory. The only thing that strikes me as a really big weakness—I never thought of it before with regard to Skidmore—is the way the buildings meet the ground. This and the landscape projects. When looked at a little closer, they are often very, very weak. They exist at the level of a gesture, which one could support, but when you look for the next level of articulation, there's nothing there. I find that remarkable, and also for the way this issue relates to high-rise buildings: how does a high-rise come down to the ground? It's as though the way in which a building comes down to the ground has almost become a non-issue, which I find astonishing.

CB: You're touching on one of the great problems in the design of high-rise buildings. You're dead right. Everyone thinks of the form from the tenth story upwards in terms of its effect on the skyline. There are very few who negotiate the ground.

KF: When all the weight comes

down to the ground, that's a dramatic moment, full of potential.

CB: But that's where artists and sculptors are not engaged enough. In architecture, the routine of the problem to solve is so huge by the time they're getting down to the designing of the base, from there on, it's transference, it's lost into the continuum of the earth, and bang it goes. I hardly think anyone spends real time negotiating contact with the ground.

JR: Yes, when artists or designers are brought in to consider that problem, the issue is already closed.

JH: Profoundly closed.

KF: This is particularly remarkable when some of the high-rises have primarily been conceived sculpturally, right?

CB: Indeed, indeed.

WW: Well, so the discussion now has reached the point where there is an ideal of looking for buildings that have a comprehensive quality at all levels, right? We've already identified different issues such as grounding, such as the tension between the exterior and normative organizational planning. I wonder whether we

should, nevertheless, hold onto this ideal of the comprehensiveness of the statement. And whether it's possible with this discussion in mind to accept that maybe none of them are going to have this kind of comprehensive quality, but that some of them are going to have more than others. I see one very interesting aspect, a kind of willingness to explore different spatial organizational forms within institutional buildings. I think the Kuwait Police College is interesting, I think the Informal Office is interesting. There are these projects that are emerging, which are different and do address how institutions, how offices, or whatever other functional type, could be rethought and therefore reshaped.

KF: Actually that's a very interesting point of departure: the way in which The Informal Office questions what office space really is and what workspace is in relation to residence.

WW: So any further thoughts, or should we go through this room and begin to select?

JH: I think it's time to put the dots on.

WW: We should make a first cut.

The point is even if we cut too much, we can always come back to review our initial decision.

CB: If one of us flags it, it stays in. If four are not interested and one says yes, we should mark it and come back and see it.

WW: Yes. I'll record the vote; if there is one vote for a scheme, we can retain it.

KF: This Hong Kong project is an example of the landscape issue I was talking about. When you compare government work to that of Skidmore, well, maybe Skidmore does it better; however, then when you look at it closely, it all disappears; it is just landscape, so the reaction is: let's paint it green.

JH: I think your landscape problem is really right, because the landscape is enormous [inaudible] it goes to the ground there, and all this ...

JR: I wonder generally if there's some problem here with the presentation versus aspiration, that there are other kinds of drawings that have to be developed and that might take us beyond the simple diagram.

KF: These drawings are pretty conventional. They're just like cal-endar sunset illustrations. Hardly on the cutting edge of landscape.

JR: There's an argument being made for preserving open space. The strongest argument would be to develop a compelling landscape to take the place of buildings.

WW: Lester Pearson, Toronto.

KF: Well, I find parts of the scheme very interesting. But when I see the plans, it's just another airport. It's no contribution to the development of the type.

JR: It looks as if the innovation was in the structural moment and in the cross section, but then it was simply extruded and laid into a normal plan.

WW: Well, I mean, in all fairness, airports are some of the most complex organizations next to hospitals.

KF: Still, I think SOM ought to be able to rethink them. I mean, if these people can't do it, who can? I just think, what is this: La Guardia revisited?

CB: There are only two types of airports: there is either the radial model with the long fingers running off to the satellites, or there is the Kansai model with the long linear run.

KF: But Foster's Hong Kong is slightly different, isn't it?

WW: Hong Kong is linear in structure, which I think we'll see in another project.

KF: Nevertheless, I think the relationship between the public perception of the space and the direction of the structure is still something fundamental that has to be resolved.

WW: There are four airports to be reviewed. Let's move on to San Francisco then. Initially, I was very much interested in the structural concept. However, I think it's highly problematic not to have these supports at the ends. In essence this is a structure that doesn't want to be supported.

CB: That's not a very interesting approach. The only interest in a spatial sense would be with these lights, like Stanstead's light wells or those at Kansai, distributing light in a line. Have you been in there?

KF: I have been in it, and I found it somewhat disorienting. However, the rhetorical use of the roof structure together with its frontal treatment of that structure in relation to the moment of arrival is very impressive.

CB: I think people in that space probably enjoy being there, but I hadn't marked this one down.

WW: I think I would support this scheme.

KF: I would vote for it.

CB: So that's two.

JH: I would wait on this. It's not the best for me, but worthy of an honorable mention simply for the fact that you could be in there and find a reason to go on living. I do find the bulging too literal and predictable.

WW: Above Net: it's an office building for an internet company plus leasable space. It's an addition to an existing building.

KF: What's behind the two-story-high screen?

JR: It's a blank façade with building services.

KF: I find this very seductive.

CB: I too found it interesting.

JR: But actually the only place that screen overlaps is in a part of the lobby, and the rest, unfortunately, is just a blank façade.

CB: It's just a screen, a veil hanging, a moiré effect.

JH: I didn't vote for it.

JR: I voted for it just because I thought the screen was seductive.

WW: Beijing City Museum.

JH: This is one of my favorites.

KF: I am for keeping it. My first one.

WW: The Guggenheim comes to Beijing in disguise.

JH: Yes, better than Bilbao.

CB: I really like the landscaping and the simple organization. This opening, the way of entering the building, had an intrigue for me that I did like.

KF: I would be interested to know how this building stands. I suppose it must be achieved by means of a Vierendeel. But there's nothing supporting it. So is it a double cantilever?

CB: That's what they're doing. These are just external wind bracers here. SOM is bringing in lots of diagonals.

KF: So the section doesn't show structure, does it?

CB: Not here.

KF: I would vote for keeping this one.

WW: Four to one.

CB: I like the organization, but I didn't like the actual structural treatment.

WW: Penn Station.

CB: This is a huge space which you enter from the side. Once entered, you see this sweeping arc which is up there near the door to the street. Then you go down into the station.

WW: I think it's an interesting attempt to separate and connect two facing buildings by creating a means of connecting different levels.

CB: I agree.

JR: I think there were some really strong constraints on the designers. They couldn't make the obvious moves of entering into the front of the Farley Building and the Post Office, so they had to make those side entries. There's a very interesting sectional move to bring people down from the tiara space to the tracks.

WW: The Informal Office, Singapore.

CB: It's the first one I marked down.

JR: The only frustration I had was the fact that there was an argument about the Robert Morris piece.

CB: Exactly, that's a weakness.

JR: It's a reductive moment.

CB: It's not clear if the project is trying to argue along the lines of

Bataille. This project is stronger if you forgot all of that and went forward with organization principles as the driving force.

JR: That's what I was saying earlier: this scheme represents a threshold moment in the way one can develop an overall pattern of space and then develop finer modulations of skin and form.

WW: Riverside South.

CB: This is what it could have been if they'd followed the zoning laws. The onyx could be interesting.

KF: It's not developed in terms of tectonics. The tectonics of the skin is also not indicated. You can't judge it because it's just graphic effect.

JR: It's a code, not material.

KF: Yes, but what is all this drawing, what is all this texture?

JR: The argument that's being made here is that this form of modulation would cover any possible internal changes that might occur.

CB: True, that's interesting, but you don't know how these people are going to move their cupboards and other pieces of furniture.

WW: I think all of these considerations come from the sixties.

The whole notion of indeterminacy. If we think of Candilis, Josic and Woods's Berlin Free University. It's now being applied to the surface. But still, I find this operation interesting.

KF: There are Europeans who have already played with this.

WW: So what's the final vote?

KF: Not me.

JH: Yes, I didn't vote for it, but I think it deserves a salute for at least trying to treat the skin in a different way. I know it's happening in Europe better and more, but still.

KF: Except you get worried about what would happen under the pressure of development. The play between these surfaces is going to be flattened out by value engineering, and then you will be left with nothing. You just have a building that's covered with some stuff, you don't have anything with a deeper complexity or interest.

WW: Let's move on to South Dearborn, this pinnacle object.

KF: What I find is that you project a building like this and you write about its structure, but you get no indication technically about how the structure connects with the space inside. So you just have to take their word for it.

CB: They're running a mast right through, and these top stories are cantilevered from the mast. So they're revealing the structure; here it hits the ground, and here you know these externals are working as a series of very few columns. It is a modern high-rise technique for very tall buildings.

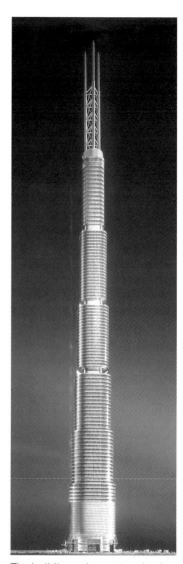

The building volume steps back to reveal the mast here, and then it carries on through, so this is a residential domain with no columns at all. I put a tick on it. If it's going to be the world's tallest building, I had to. But I think it's such a powerful statement. They could have done more, I agree with Ken, and I'm not sure about their idea. They say in the text that they wanted to reveal their hand on the upper thirty stories, and it's just a simple core building shafted with piers. Actually more is happening in here to make the world's tallest building.

KF: A visible megastructure always can be used to modulate the scale of a very high building. But here it seems most of the structure is always covered with a skin, so there is never a possibility for modulation.

CB: Here's a simple symbolic move to say "telescope." Mast and telescope. You pull your antennae up, that's what the architect is doing.

KF: Yes, but that is an industrial design metaphor.

CB: I'd give it a vote because it's the tallest building and I think they made the effort here. But, there are very weak moments. For example this little apron.

KF: Terrible.

CB: Really, that is very, very weak. It lets down the whole idea.

WW: So we've got two votes for this?

CB: It wasn't one of my starred ones, but I have to vote for it.

WW: Dubai Airport.

KF: What's the relationship between the structure and space? I find it very unconvincing. The exterior form of the structure produces what?

JR: It produces the design.

KF: It's not very aesthetic from a plastic standpoint.

JR: The exterior doesn't really reveal itself in a clear way, either.

CB: There is something quite elegant here I'd like to bring to

your attention. These structural elements are quite flappy things, so they had to be tied down. They have tied them down vertically using cable stays. The structural engineer has done a decent job, but it's very minimal. More could have been done, particularly in Dubai.

WW: The Cathedral.

KF: I'm a sucker for this one.

WW: Me too.

KF: I feel it is very promising, but I don't quite know where it is placed.

JR: In a way it's not even about the structural honesty.

CB: The danger was not to produce images of prayer and clasping hands like the monument in Bagdad.

KF: But the luminous interiors at the bottom are interesting.

JH: That's the best part.

CB: This is a problem with big firms. You get the references and the metaphors, all very interesting. The translation into the details that actually makes poetry versus the pedestrian or the mundane is very difficult because big forces run through big companies. It's an organizational problem. I live

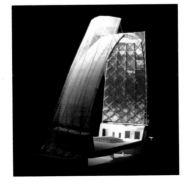

with it all that all the time too.

KF: Something odd is going on here isn't it? You ask yourself why this is not just one structure.

JR: This is more about a superposition of structures and skins, but they're not really integrated.

CB: I thought it lost an opportunity. That's why I didn't vote for it.

JR: My hope was that it wasn't about some kind of structural honesty, but that it was about trying to produce new spatial effects through superimposed layering.

JH: It's an opportunity missed.

WW: Two votes? Two.

WW: The revisiting of Lever House.

KF: I find it fantastic, very good. They did a great job. Let's go on.

CB: I don't think enough is being said. This is the end product. A component of the beauty of Lever House is the interior and its organization of the fifties, and this seems to be the answer reflecting that, but that's all it is. It doesn't convince me.

WW: It's interesting that this is the headquarters for Alcoa. Given that, there's a lot of wood in it.

KF: A bit too much wood.

WW: The explanatory text is all about transparency, democracy, and no hierarchy, yet in the end there are still the boss's offices in the corners complete with glass doors.

WW: Democracy through the glass door, right? So it has no …

JH: Relevance.

WW: Sustainable Housing in Tai Ho.

KF: I thought that was worth a vote.

WW: You thought it was sustainable.

KF: Well, I didn't think too much about the issue of sustainability, but I was interested by the fact that an office like this makes an effort to integrate a large residential development into a larger landscape. It looks to me like a serious effort.

CB: I didn't vote for it because sustainability here is just the openness of the landscape.

WW: I can see an attempt to involve the terrain. But I'm deeply suspicious when it comes to the notion of sustainable residential development on this scale because it will have a tremendous effect on the microclimate and the ground water level given these large, multistory buildings.

WW: Let's gather round this one here, Ben Gurion Airport.

KF: The awkward joints don't surface in this rendering because the representation is dematerialized.

WW: Again, it's similar to the other airports where the actual scope of possible development is very limited, the approach is defensive. All the security, the organizational requirements, customs,

and so forth need to be solved, so that what one looks at has those kinds of gestures in mind. While I find it interesting, I don't think it's all that significant. I'd be more interested in how one could get a more efficient type working given this requirement of going through the center, something which in the United States is different because you have much larger airports.

JR: One wonders why the whole building is broken up into blocks when it's possible to make one large envelope that would not have such strange choked intersections.

KF: There also seems to be not as much thought given to the expansion of the airport, at least judging from the drawings.

WW: The AIG Tower in Hong Kong.

CB: Here, again, I think a trick is missed. This looked interesting where you're opening up, but then you don't see anything.

WW: This is the development of this object. These references to lanterns and sailboats are very interesting.

CB: But that's a weakness.

JR: References kill the project.

KF: There are two issues here. One has to do with references and the other has to do with the way the building is lit. I'm struck over and over again how beautifully Rockefeller Center is lit. This project, however, is of the kind that wants to tell you that above all it's going to be a light display, but then the actual light proposal is not convincing at all.

JR: Well, it's a Photoshop tool, it's just lens flare superimposed upon the building.

WW: Algarve Stadium. I like the organizational idea, the flexibility of the seating. I'm not convinced at all by the forms. I don't think that they are structurally considered.

CB: What I didn't like about it again is that there is a huge opportunity lost in the design of the structure. If you design a free form like this and start to break up the form, then the structure's got to do more than stick in a series of marks at the same angle running throughout with only the two main verticals. This should have been integral.

WW: There are some seats which are removable and capable of being recycled. So it can actually be made much more intimate for less intensive uses.

WW: Ascot Racecourse.
CB: I gave a vote for this, again this isn't one of my starters. There was an attempt being made here.
KF: The roof is just too exaggerated.
WW: I'm intrigued by it, because it doesn't relate to anything.
CB: I liked the idea of introducing a berm into the grounds, I'm not sure that this would work. This could integrate with the people, but it has to be extended.
KF: The problem is that there is no integration. I assume that these four layers are VIP boxes. Then there's another layer lower down; a perfect model of English society, right there.
CB: I couldn't understand the structure in relation to the form. I'm not sure if someone's cheating here.
KF: There seem to be two different structures.
WW: But then, how does the structure really work?
CB: I have no idea. Well, it certainly shouldn't work like that. That's for sure. It's wrong, really wrong designwise. There's a contradic-tory structural and formal language, here's a Cartesian post and beam language with flowing sails, and this is supposed to be the galloping horse's mane. They should be more interlocking in their form, and to engage the ground, it would be much more powerful. Something could have been made with that. If you use a free form like this, which is very powerful, it should be an integrated scheme.
KF: Well, the project consists of two different structural propositions, comprising in part a system of columns.
CB: The berm idea was good, but didn't understand enough of it. I did give it a vote because I liked the berm idea.
JR: The berm idea was what I liked.
CB: One vote. It has my vote.

WW: We come to Logan Terminal E.
JR: This was a bit of a mystery to me: lanterns in space.
KF: I find them intriguing.
JR: My wish was that the whole building did that.
WW: It's back to the issue of the normative frame, this time with modulated shapes inserted.
CB: I gave it a vote.
KF: I gave it a vote.

JH: I give it a vote too. I wish they'd done more, and more thoroughly, but even with that, this one seems to have some considerations for intriguing lighting.
KF: It also allows for sunlight during the day.
JR: You can almost imagine a junior staff member designing the lanterns.
WW: For purposes of adding retail to the terminal, extending it by some forty feet, a steel structure containing all these things is being constructed. In essence, the whole of Logan Airport is being reshaped to include overhead connectors and people movers.
CB: If they can do what they are saying in the text, it will be nice.

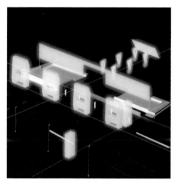

WW: Academic Landscape, Greenwich Academy.
KF: A very interesting text, but I'm not convinced by the drawings. The words sound great, but I couldn't see evidence of what they are talking about. Above all, a chronic lack of sections.
JR: Still there was an attempt to look at models that bring together maps and buildings.
JR: I put a vote in for it just

because it seemed to me to move beyond the normative in some way. They're really trying to deal with normative building envelopes and the interpenetration of their lower elements into roofscapes.

WW: One vote, okay.

WW: Cablenet Entrance.

CB: I couldn't see how the entrance relates to the building. That was my problem. If it's by itself you have to judge it as a real piece of corporate structure. It's a good attempt, it's one where you get a good expression of primary strength there; all this filigree work is standard.

KF: I think it's good, but there are two things that phenomenologically or perceptually seem to be absent. One is the glass panels themselves, and two is, where is it? I mean, what kind of a contextual situation are we in?

CB: That's the problem, lack of context.

JR: I think even in the overall frame, there's a constraining element. It's not a very good one to my mind. It's a way of updating a portal in the most obvious way. So you have a high-tech portal, but

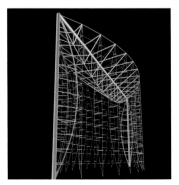

it's still a portal.

KF: It's almost like a portal you can't get through.

CB: I can't see how the building works. Maybe in here. Maybe the entrance is here, you go through here.

WW: Votes?

CB: I had one vote because, well, you know, I like this image.

JR: Yes, actually it's interesting, it's the image, it's the fragment that is more holistic than the overall form.

CB: Yes, this doesn't convince me at all, this is La Villette gone worse, it's too much of it. So we can judge it as a piece of structure which is sculpture, and it's wanting. It could be far more refined. That's a heroic attempt to just make that, but that jump should be very important and fully integrated—is that seamless or what? That's the expression. All the rest of it is an enormous effort to keep that one line in space, and then it's not successful.

WW: Kuwait Police College.

KF: I find this to be a very intriguing project.

CB: I like the potential, I starred it as one of my better ones. I tried not to get seduced by these images.

WW: I find the organization interesting, the way that these elements are beginning to be transformed topologically and in the end also to drive the form.

JR: There is not only the organizational model, but there's also an experiential and perceptual thing going on with the light wells and spaces …

KF: There are subliminal messages throughout.

JR: And also the Turrell light room.

WW: How Turrell figures light …

JH: Well, that's the part that's sinister. That the Police College is so aesthetically appealing. That's worrisome to me, although I liked the building very much.

JR: It is problematic. If it were out in Colorado Springs …

JH: If it were a meditation center …

WW: Is there unanimous vote? Are you voting for it?

JH: Yes, I'll vote for it.

WW: 350 Madison Avenue, this kind of reshaping of an existing building. Putting the old façade on a shelf, so to speak.

KF: It is actually superior to what we have seen before.

JR: I'll vote for this.

JR: Of course this is the desired final image.

WW: But in a way, the project is unfinished, so this image is a commentary that everything is about planning.

KF: In relation to this surface, you wonder what was the spatial potential there? There is no indication. The revelation of the interior to the street could be amazing.

JR: You mean that the gap between the buildings becomes internal to the building itself.

KF: Even if the scheme is only about the elevator banks, all the elevators moving at the same time, that could really have been something to see. In any event it gets my vote.

WW: Singapore Airport.

JH: I liked this one, particularly the butterfly roof.

JR: I must say I'm completely taken by it.

WW: I think it's fantastic. It must be a nightmare for them to get to this stage.

CB: I wonder whether it could really be this real. It would probably never be like that. It will be something different. It raises issues: is this decoration, is it ornament? Does it function? It's all of those issues in different ways.

JH: Very few of the things we're seeing have been as comprehensive as this one.

JR: I would have to support it whether or not it even works in this project yet, and I think that the direction of experimentation in the office has to be commended.

WW: I agree. Your comment earlier on, if it's not SOM, then who? A small practice could never convince a large client to undertake a scheme like this one.

CB: Right, SOM could convince a client to build these flaps. I think they will be more utilitarian.

KF: What most worries me is the quality of the space other than the three dimensional pyrotechnics of the roof.

JR: That's all it is.

CB: This is the problem we've got with these huge airports or big façades. You take the whole surface and then jazz it up. There's a functional element here, with the louvers and sun working together.

WW: 200 Broadway, folding and unfolding.

JR: This had my vote. The reason why is that there was at least an attempt to try to make spatial some of the issues that were brought up today with the modulation projects. It's still very diagrammatic, very dematerialized. But this is one of the first instances where there is some experimentation in terms of how to deal with a large series of volumes on a ground space. So it isn't a norma-

tive landscape project. They're attempting to make multiple grounds that connect to the base. It begins to answer some of the criticisms that were set out earlier.

KF: You have a feeling you're dealing with some kind of deception here.

CB: How are we going to proceed with the selected schemes?

WW: I was thinking that we could go for six. I would make a plea for diversity of types, and I would also make a plea for reexamining some of the votes here or, shall we say, ignoring the votes to have more or less equals and then to assess them on their merits as a vote of finalists, so to speak. We can have different opportunities with different kinds of objects or projects. Each offers a certain amount of leeway and innovation. Maybe there are some schemes which have more profound contributions to make to the world of architecture than others. On that scale one would select some schemes rather than others?

CB: I think if we take Wilfried's idea, which I think is a good one, we would start our process again. We would just talk through what we see in them and vote again. I could pick three that I really like above the others. If we do that in this round, then we come down to say five or six.

WW: Before we do that, let's categorize types. Infrastructural projects. Let's group them and let's talk about those together.

CB: Since SOM has asked us to judge their designs, we should be judging the genre, the type of building, and then the question should be asked: what does it contribute to the world of architecture?

WW: The issues in the case of airports are actually quite similar.

KF: San Francisco is more like one of the airports designed by von Gerkan and Marg.

CB: Yes, big signs of structure. I don't think it does much for organizing space.

WW: This is an attractive form, but I

don't think it really accounts for the structural system. Its relationship to the supports is problematic.

JR: Even then there's a difference between this diagram and how the envelope is finally involved.

CB: Yes, these columns would disappear in the organization of the form internally. I'm sure there are huge partition walls going up.

WW: Penn Station is also different because the project is working within an existing building. This is quite a difficult issue in terms of operability while construction takes place. It is quite a difference to a new building.

JR: Part of the attraction of Penn Station too is just the understanding of the number of constraints relative to that site and what it

was possible to do. So in a way it seems less about the architecture per se than about the field of limitations that they had to work with to achieve it. The Singapore project really begins to point the way towards another direction for the practice. It seems part of the lineage of the new skin vocabulary on the towers, but it then takes it further and begins to suggest that one could even begin to modulate zones in space.

WW: These two projects form a structural research, underlining what Jesse said. The Logan scheme, well, the trouble is I use this airport regularly; I've seen this happening over the last few months and years …

KF: You haven't seen one of the proposed lanterns yet, have you?

WW: I haven't seen a lantern yet. I have seen the other things which do exactly that kind of pattern of the different glazing elements enshrouding either these structural cores or these staircase elevators. And I felt that they were …

CB: Distracting, rather than telling of their construction. These are supposed to be sculptural 3D forms coming out of here and lit from the ground.

JR: It's funny, because in the end

the building itself is somewhat retrograde relative to the invention.

CB: Yes, that's what puzzles me.

WW: That's why Singapore is much more coherent. It has a statement about how indirect light can enter through the roof rather than occupying a space with object lights. Logan Airport is ingenious; I'm not saying it's not clever.

JR: In a sense the Singapore project is more ideological in its direction. It takes one beyond a move that molds the gross form in a building. Here the position is that you can take regular elements and by running them through a variational field, you can produce that difference without having to make shapes. I think that's very interesting.

WW: It's remarkable because we all know Singapore's self-understanding, and for the client, a city such as Singapore requires quite a lot of convincing by the architect to do something like this. So we come back to the issue: what authority does an architect have in order to develop a standard type?

JH: In defense of Logan, I don't think the building is all that remarkable, but I still have to salute the lighting because it's been so neglected throughout; in a way it's very economical, effective, and coherent, producing a unifying result with an economy of means.

CB: I look at it from the commoner's point of view as well. These airports are huge spaces, except the terminal for Logan. In the case of Penn Station, the movement is obvious, there is a big cascade. People using this station will feel something extra happening with the architecture affecting them. There is something in that project for me. Equally the Singapore project is potentially interesting with a huge field of planes.

JH: It's not about control.

CB: I go for Penn Station and Singapore.

WW: Alright, let's go through the other schemes.

JH: I still like the Beijing Museum because it has a number of things that are interesting, even if it's Guggenheim related. I like the logic of the ramp. I think that corner is dramatic, but not gratuitously so; it seems to be respectable enough, it seems to add something new.

WW: I would have liked to have seen more of the context. There is nothing to indicate that. That's a pity. We know that Beijing is changing daily, so, under these circumstances, maybe the lack of context is not that significant. However, the museum is located between the first and the second traffic network. So we're still in the traditional part of the city.

JR: Right, but this museum tries to produce its own context. The building is made up of a few sub-buildings, some of which would appear as extended from an image of that context. Then there is this large cantilevering element, the main block being somehow the newest piece, even though they're all the same age. It troubles me that in designing

the bracketing elements the architects feel the need to rein-scribe what's already there.

KF: What do you mean?

JR: The two masonry structures appear to be buildings that existed prior to the main volume, and they code into the context so that they would appear more continuous with it.

KF: The thing that is very unfortunate about it is the relationship between those buildings and the spiral, and the fact that the way the load is transmitted is partly concealed. I don't like that at all. In trying to assess this work one is once again caught up with the conceptual and landscape aspects of it. The conception of the landscape is perhaps the strongest aspect. It's like a project that didactically offers two sides which make it interesting. There's the positive and the negative side of it, but you don't quite understand why these masonry buildings are so dumb, so to speak. I can understand being driven toward some kind of contrast, but they didn't have to make them quite so incoherent.

WW: Well, I think it is a reference to the Forbidden City.

KF: Even so, does it have to be neo-plasticized? I mean the actual Forbidden City is not neo-plasticized. In formal terms,

this gesture is very gratuitous.

WW: This design embraces "both/and"; it's a reflection of tradition and a fusion with modernism, so to speak.

KF: Please.

JR: Post-modernism. That's the post-modern element.

KF: Yes it is.

JR: It is about the necessity to make references.

WW: Yes, you could imagine the thinking that went along with it. This is the way that most architects tend to ground their decisions.

JH: I don't think it's that clumsy. It just seems to say this to me in a somewhat obvious way, but I don't think it's desperate.

WW: It expresses what I think the city authorities would like to see, this emergence from a tradition to something very …

KF: With it.

WW: Modern. Yes. In the same way that the French authorities have always been interested in the British high-tech because they have felt rather inferior. That thinking always plays a role in the way something as direct and straightforward as this juxtaposition might come about. Alright, should we look at the offices? One office? Or two?

KF: I would fight for keeping both

of them given this conversation about the role of developers.

CB: The 350 Madison scheme attempts to do something in order to keep the developer happy.

KF: Right, and the Singapore scheme, I don't know if it's an absolutely remarkable plan, but I find it a very intriguing project all the same.

WW: Well, I would be more inclined to let the Madison scheme go. The Singapore scheme is the most comprehensive.

KF: It surely is, and these are big

developers, vis-à-vis the issue of developers and their supposed limitations.

CB: Putting up towers in New York.

JR: And it's very interesting too when you compare the 350 Madison building with the building in China, I suspect that the façade is not something that was the choice of the architect, but a requirement for the site. And it's made quite clear in the way that the existing façade is treated.

CB: I think the design intent behind this is clear. You see what they're trying to do. But the Singapore office is better.

JR: It is better.

KF: No doubt about it.

WW: Okay. We have to make a selection out of the glass projects.

JR: Do we have to choose from one of these or can we put them together as a project, as joint research?

KF: I would suggest we put them together.

CB: Yes.

JR: They don't really represent finished projects as much as investigations.

KF: I would prefer to put them together. What I think is unique here is that we are being presented with the fragments of a system. We don't get the whole.

JR: It's also the message we're sending to SOM. It isn't the choice of a project, but I think we have to support that direction of thought and experimentation.

KF: What I think is interesting is that the different pieces show a systematic capacity. Although this work is not stunningly original, it's carried out with incredible sensitivity with regard to the manner in which the pieces are put together.

CB: But is this all glass crystal? I mean it says crystalline glass. What I like about it is the ambiguity; it's like a typewriter.

JH: It's like an insect, like a spring. I appreciate the implied movement, it looks like it could crouch.

KF: But it also suggests to me that above all there's a lot of structural skill. I find it very intriguing.

WW: Now, we've done a review of the schemes that we have left. The aim now is to find six. We have nine schemes, and we ought to go through with a vote on each.

KF: Can we not talk about possible elimination cases?

WW: Yes.

KF: I would like to start a discussion, I would be for eliminating San Francisco Airport.

CB: I'd go along with that.

CB: I think this has more to say.

WW: We'll definitely leave out San Francisco. I'm also for eliminating Logan Airport.

KF: Singapore is attempting to find another language.

CB: But it's not proven, is it?

WW: No, it's not proven.

KF: Well, we are judging the drawings.

JR: In the end, the lanterns at Logan would be tremendously interesting as building envelopes themselves, but as mere lanterns they fall back into conventional models …

CB: This might just be cosmetic on the end, whereas Singapore would really organize the flow of people.

KF: Singapore is the most aesthetic scheme. This is where you get a dialectic between movement and a dumb building.

JR: In a way I would have wanted an even dumber building. This building is sort of a straight jacket around the elements within.

CB: There's no meaning. Penn Station and Singapore are better.

JR: Absolutely. There's no question in my mind. And Singapore really suggests models of many different scales for future work.

It's really potent, although it's still constrained to the realm of light effects.

JH: This could transform any number of municipal buildings in the world. It would be relatively cheap and easy. I think San Francisco is out for me.

WW: Is that unanimous then?

KF: For me it is also out.

JH: Out.

WW: You want to keep it? You want to vote for it?

JR: I would support it over Logan, actually. I mean you're talking about buildings.

WW: Let's vote on Penn Station. Who's in favor of keeping it in?

CB: I keep it.

WW: ... two, three. We'll keep Singapore too.

JR: To me that's Best in Show.

JH: I agree.

WW: Logan? One, two, three votes against. Three to two. Beijing City Museum.

CB: Not me, anymore. This basic idea is good, but we are trying to eliminate. It's hard. I like the idea, I just don't like the result.

WW: That's three to two then. So it's out. Are we unanimous on the Informal Office?

CB: Yes. So unanimous on Kuwait too.

JH: I am not completely there with the architecture. I just have to note in passing that the combination of all these Turrell chambers with the rigors of paramilitary training, that's somewhere between funny and sinister.

JR: Indeed, Turrell was a U2 pilot.

JH: Yes, so the world's complicated, but I just think that's problematic.

WW: Okay, what about the glass projects? Did we make a decision on these?

KF: I would vote to keep it in.

CB: I take Ken's point, but in our comments we're recommending that team.

KF: Why I am so impressed is because, within the paradoxical climate of the United States which is always perceived to be the most modern country in the world, really competent, technical work in architecture is very rare, particularly when it is combined

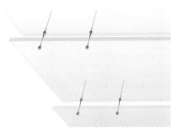

with a poetic dimension. There is no high-tech American architecture, strictly speaking.

WW: That's true, and I think it's important to recognize it. Airports and other kinds of infrastructural projects usually suffer from the stuff in between the terminals. The terminals are user-driven, and they're funded partly by that, and the stuff in between is usually thrown away. Forgotten. I imagine the budget for these projects was relatively limited. It looks like a more than decent result.

JR: So the only question is the tower.

CB: Well, SOM's work with towers, and we should have a tower.

KF: A tower subject to the ruthless laws of the monstrous Manhattan real estate market.

JH: Did the world's tallest building get at least three votes on the first round?

WW: No, the South Dearborn Chicago high-rise received only two votes.

JH: I remembered incorrectly. I thought it had three votes rather than two votes.

CB: I think for completeness's sake we should return to the marginals.

WW: Let's go through all these things and see if there's anything we missed.

JH: Last chance.

WW: And there is the Columbus Circle scheme.

CB: With all the high-rises on the table, it's a test, isn't it? Take the old context, shoot up, make something sculptural, give it a façade treatment. Yes, I had a vote for it.

JR: But is there anything really novel about that?

CB: Not really. One vote for that?

JH: Yes, I do.

WW: We'll correct this to a three-to-two vote. Okay, so we have done justice to the high-rise, and we have found one, and that will form our sixth entry.

WW: So let's have the final vote, those in favor of keeping it in.

CB: I'll keep it in. I like that grain.

WW: Okay, so finally we have six schemes?

KF: Logan has fallen off the table. I'm sorry to see Logan go. Well, we're done.

WW: I would like to thank you all very much. It's now three o'clock. All the comments have been recorded and will be used against you.

Renovation and Addition, Pennsylvania Station

New York, New York

Designed 1998–2001

Pennsylvania Station is America's busiest transportation facility today, serving a half million people daily—more passengers than New York's three major airports combined and more than twice the ridership of Grand Central Station. The activity of buying tickets and waiting for and boarding trains takes place in a confusing maze of corridors that are all that remains of the great McKim, Mead & White station that stood from 1900 until 1963. To remedy this condition the Pennsylvania Station Redevelopment Corporation was formed to build an expansion to the station utilizing space in the James A. Farley Post Office. The post office is a landmark building designed by McKim, Mead & White in a similar style to Penn Station. It is immediately to the west of the station and above the rail platforms. In 1935 an addition doubled the size of the building to 1.4 million square feet with a footprint as large as any structure in Manhattan, but it remains largely inaccessible to the public since it houses postal processing facilities.

To convert roughly 30 percent of the largely nonpublic post office into a rail station some modifications will be made to its exterior. The 40-foot-wide moats surrounding the building that originally were used to ventilate the rail tracks will be reduced by 30 feet, making the buildings approachable from Thirty-first and Thirty-third Streets. In the resulting plaza areas at the Eighth Avenue street corners, minor entrances to the station will be built. Their lightweight steel and glass canopies make them recognizable, but do not challenge the powerful sweep of stairs leading to the post office. The primary station entrances will be built at mid-block on Thirty-first and Thirty-third Streets with covered taxi drop-offs and facilities similar to an airport terminal curbside.

Above the main entrances rises a 150-foot-tall steel and glass shell structure that announces the new station. This structure houses the intermodal hall, which is the primary civic space in the building. Ticketing for travel by rail and air will take place in this 350-by-100-foot crescent-shaped room. The shell is a section of a sphere distorted in plan to conform to the existing building structure on which it is supported. If extended, the resulting dome would embrace the entire original post office edifice. As a fragment, the shell reaches to the east, catching the view of pedestrians on the side streets as they approach the station and orienting them towards the train room and platforms once inside. To distinguish the shell, which is intended to function as a space-defining form, from the eastern enclosure of the hall, which by contrast appears to be open, its double-layer structure is clad in fritted glass. The eastern enclosure has a single layer of structure made stable by its double curvature and is clad in clear low-iron glass. By day the ceramic frit coating on the shell helps cut glare from the western sun, while at night it absorbs artificial light to give the station a luminous presence in the city. The train room is the next in the series of spaces as one moves down toward the tracks from the intermodal hall. Also accessible directly from Eighth Avenue, it occupies the original mail sorting room in the post office. Exposed heavy steel trusses

15 feet deep that have been restored and stripped of their ornamental cladding span the 35,000-square-foot space. They are enclosed by a new glass skylight that has an integral system of glare control louvers. The existing floors beneath the skylight will be cut away to yield a tall space with a cascading profile that leads passengers down to the trains. The entire east façade of the room is a programmable media wall that provides train schedules, weather, news, and entertainment. Below this wall is a glazed area that reveals the activity at platform level and allows a broad band of daylight to reach the tracks, guiding arriving passengers to the new station.

The Pennsylvania Station Redevelopment proposes an architecture that is appropriate in scale to its internal function, but acknowledges its local and even global impact. The public uses in the building and the improvements made to the vehicular circulation around it will have a positive effect on the value of buildings on adjoining sites that have languished in the shadow of the post office. Development on the West Side rail yards two blocks away, which comprise two of the largest unimproved parcels in the city, becomes more plausible with the advent of the new station. The station has always been an urban gateway linking local subway and bus routes to a regional and national rail network; expanded, it will include airport access giving it a global dimension.

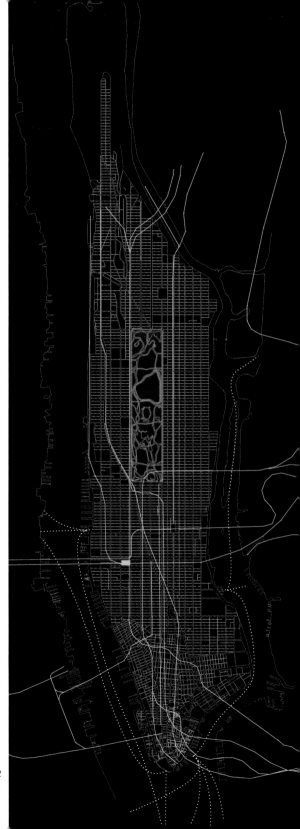

2

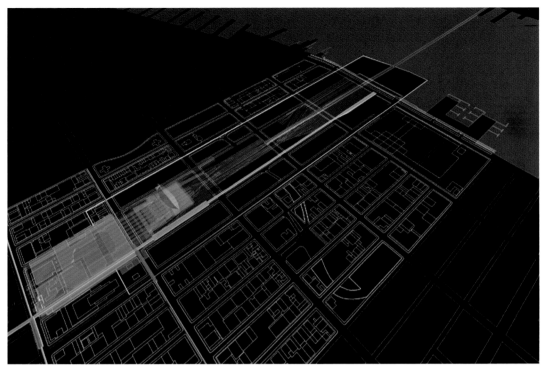

3

4

< 1 Aerial view of context

2 Map of transit links

3 Local infrastructure

4 Farley Post Office, circa 1913

> 5 New Penn Station from the east

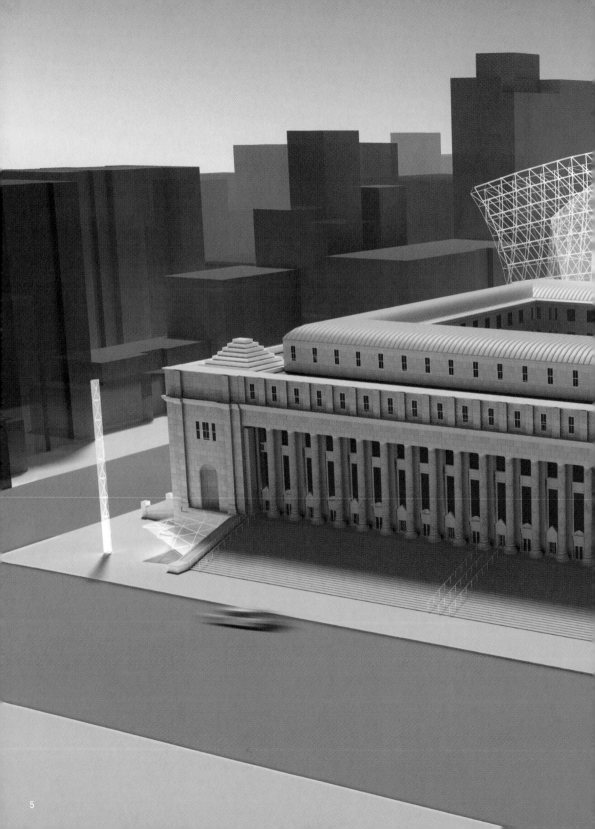

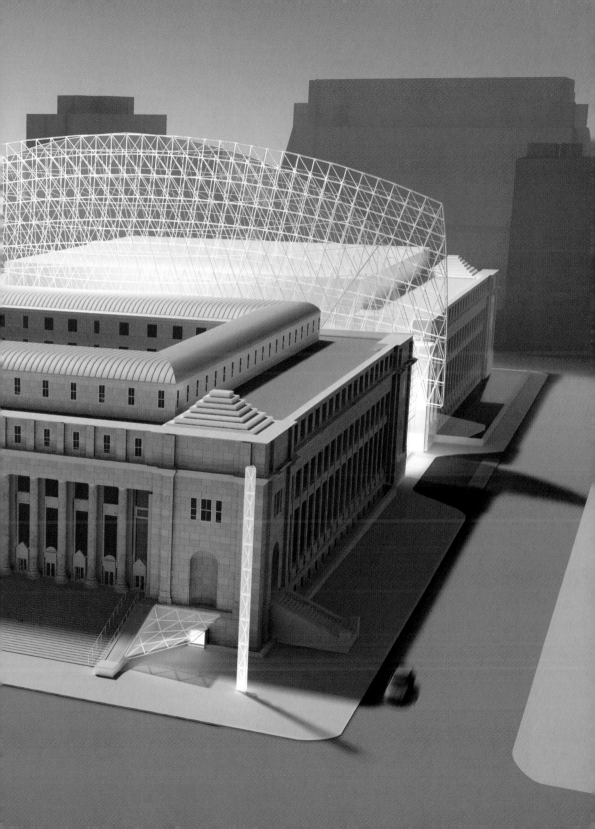

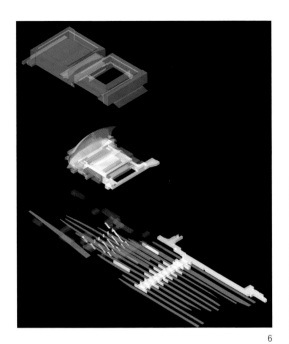

6

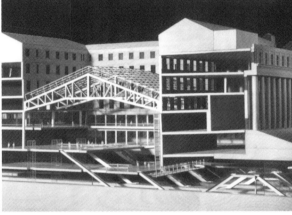

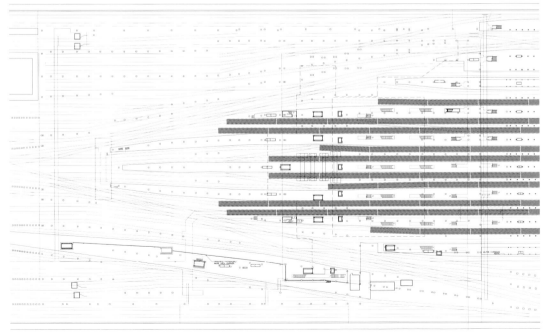

8

9

6 Diagram of uses within building
7 Section model showing connection to tracks
8 Track and platform plan
9 View to train hall from platform
10 Lower concourse plan

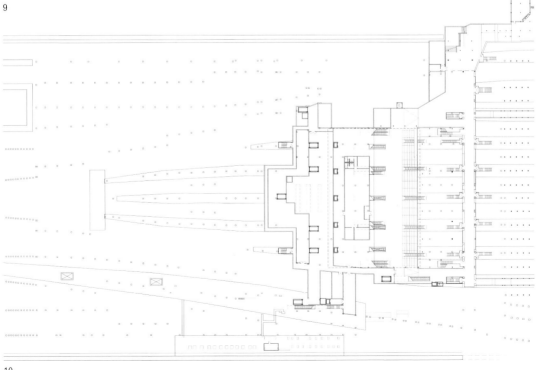

10

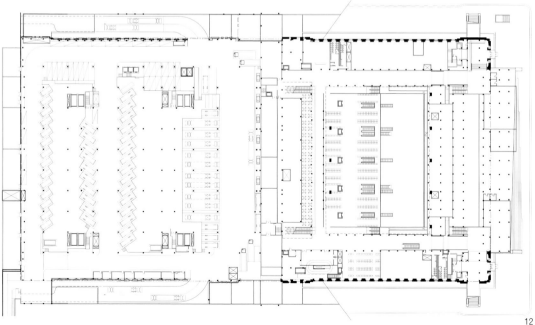

11 Existing truss under construction, circa 1912

12 Concourse plan

13 View of train hall showing refurbished truss

14 Diagram of train hall related to tracks and shell structure

15 Study of train hall from track level

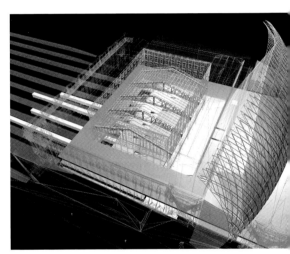

13

14

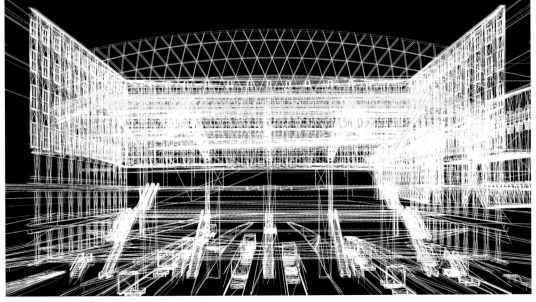

15

16 Section model of train hall
17 Section model of train hall
   media wall
18 View of media wall
19 East-west section from Eighth
   Avenue to Ninth Avenue
20 Study of new skylight
   on existing trusses

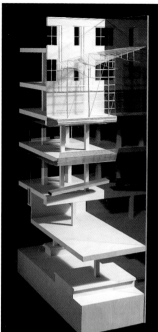

16

17

18

19

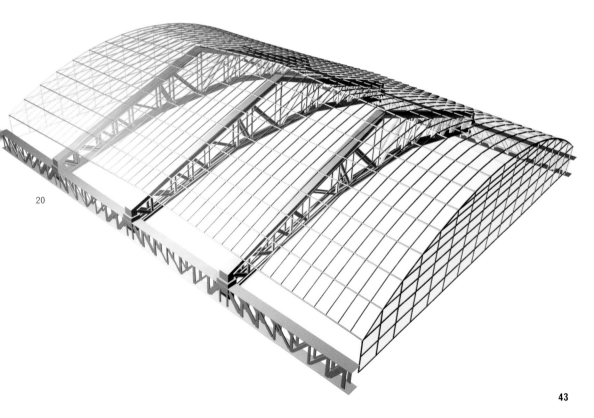

20

21 East elevation of ticketing hall
22 First floor plan
23 View of ticketing hall
24 Study model of new zinc cladding of east façade of ticketing hall
25 Diagram of relationship between shell structure and circulation down to platforms

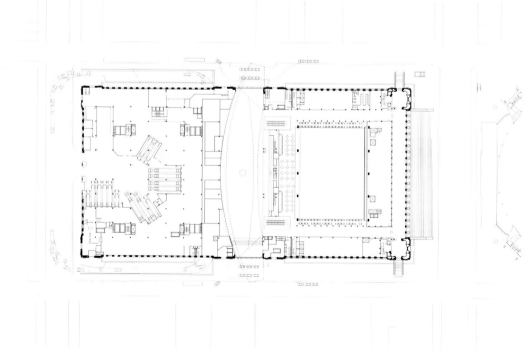

22

44

23

24

26

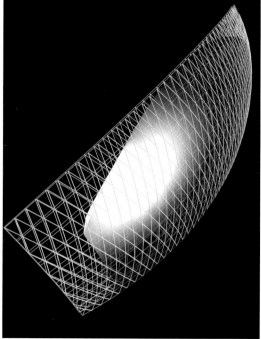

27

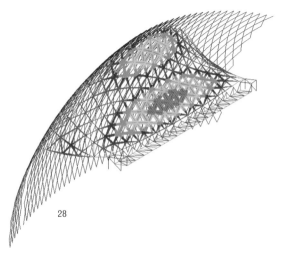

28

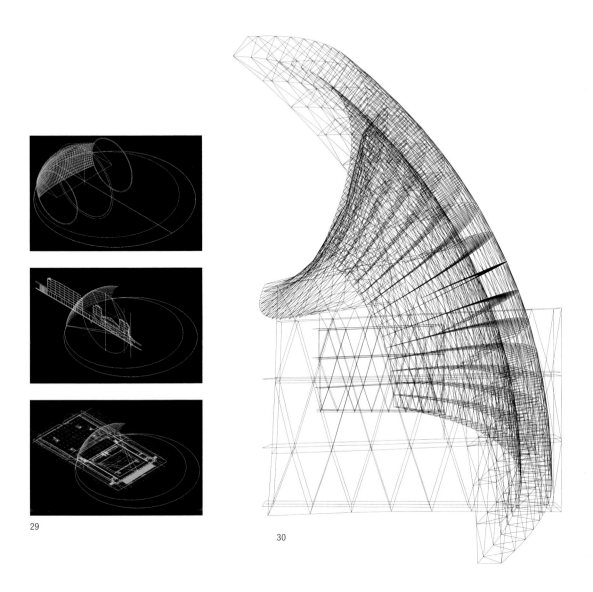

29

30

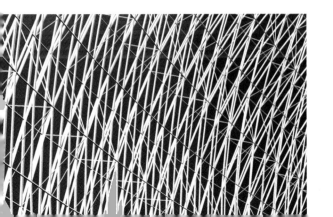

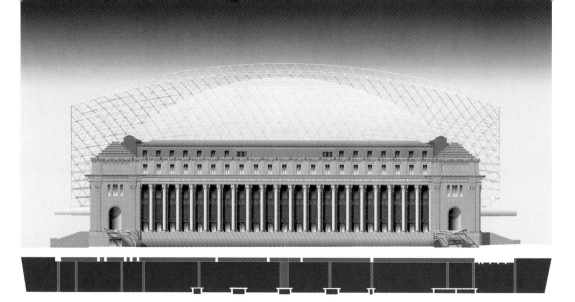

32

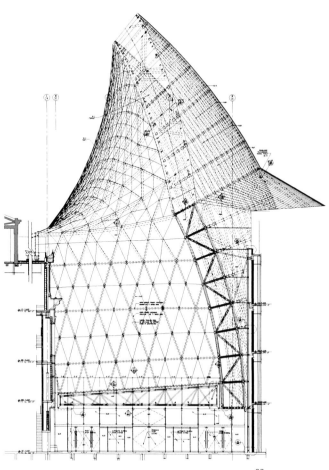

33

34

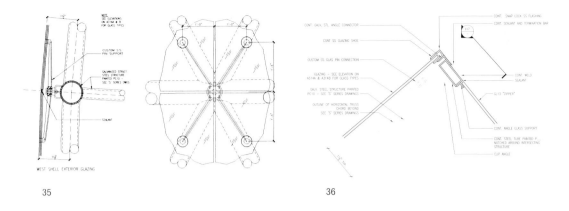

WEST SHELL EXTERIOR GLAZING

35

36

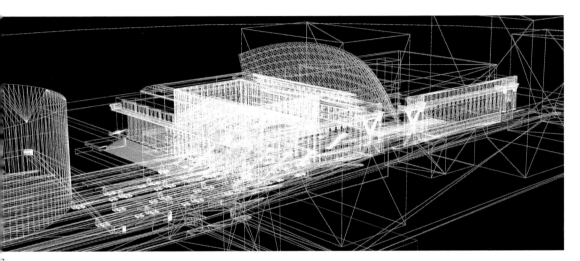

37

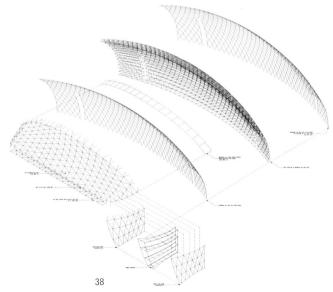

38

32 East elevation of new station

33 Construction drawing of north
    entrance

34 Study model of north entrance

35 Typical detail of glass support

36 Typical detail of glass termination

37 Study of shell structure as insert-
    ed in post office

38 Exploded diagram of shell
    components

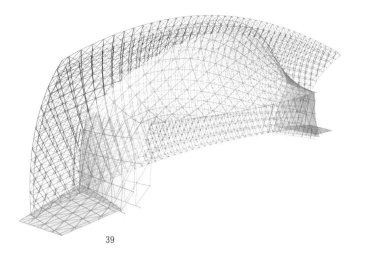

39

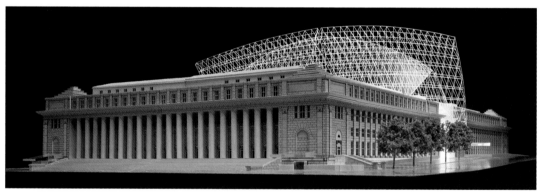

40

39 Shell and east elevation structure
40 Model photograph from Eighth
    Avenue and Thirty-third Street
41 Study model of Eighth Avenue and
    Thirty-third Street entrance
42 Thirty-third Street entrance

41

Training Facility, Kuwait Police College

Kuwait City, Kuwait

Designed 1998–2000

Kuwait City is one of the hottest inhabited cities on Earth. The landscape is a desert comprised of harsh sun, intense heat, and very fine beige sand that seems to be suspended in the air.

In the wake of the Gulf War, the need in Kuwait for a symbol of strength was paramount—an important step in rebuilding confidence. In this climate, the government of Kuwait elected to expand its police college. Currently the college is located 7 kilometers from the center of old Kuwait Town, towards the western edge of Kuwait City. The site for the new college is adjacent to their existing campus and will comprise an area of 304,284 square meters. The new complex will serve as the main campus for 1,200 elite officers, with facilities for living, academics, administration, athletics, and training. The police college is a paramilitary facility sited deliberately within the proximity of the central city; its location provides a sense of security for the inhabitants of the city.

The new college is required to be completely enclosed by a perimeter wall. The desert climate, the tradition of pre-Islamic and Islamic architecture, and the rigors and orthodoxies of training guide the design. We divided the site into five quadrants, one for each of the college's core functions described above—living, academics, administration, athletics, and training. We then divided the program of the college into two types of buildings: background buildings ("rope" buildings) that define space and special object buildings ("vessel" buildings) that capture space. The differences between these two types of buildings are expressed in their forms and constructions.

The rope buildings house the repetitive programmatic functions: classrooms, dormitories, and administration modules. They define the edges of spaces in the quadrant-oriented master plan and connect the major courtyard areas. Conceived as three-story modular units, they interlock to form a network of connected inside spaces. Bearing walls of stacked and interlocking precast concrete units 60 centimeters deep are woven into a puzzle-like pattern that allow for window apertures over 10 percent of the façade to minimize infiltration of sunlight and heat. The wall and window surfaces are planar so as not to collect the airborne sand. These concrete units are arranged in three ways to solve a specific window configuration for each building function, letting light into the rooms at different vertical heights to illuminate and support the activities within. The concrete wall assemblies include four basic precast panel shapes: S, C, L, and I. Each shape has a varying percentage of crushed glass to create a shimmering luminous effect and, when combined with the sand in the air, will create the impression of a mirage. Contained within the rope buildings are ten cubic and distinct light chambers. Each chamber is an interior volume within the larger rope building enclosure; the 1,5-meter cavity between the two captures and directs natural light from the sky into each chamber. These chambers form the entrances to each rope building and present the only path of vertical movement. The lighting of the spaces was designed in collaboration with the artist James Turrell. His focus was to create a light threshold (made of fiber optic and neon) in each unique chamber.

He has entitled the ten chambers *Sky-Pond, Aperture-Square, Eclipse, Void-Circle, Slit Scan, Big Screen, Sculptural, Big Mac, Untitled,* and *Big Open.* In contrast to the regimented and repetitive rope buildings, the vessel buildings are singular and distinctive in form. The vessel buildings house the assembly functions: mosque, auditorium, dining hall, library, and natatorium. These structures serve as structural markers in the landscape and, together with each building's associated courtyard space, provide their own sense of procession through continuity of material surface. For instance: the vessel buildings are continuous surfaces that fold to capture edges, middles, or ends of monumental space. Most surfaces (floor, wall, door, and roof) within each building are largely made of the same material; the edges where the distinct folds meet allow light to enter and escape from the space. Each paired vessel building and space, kept separate by the rope buildings, is legible by material. The dining hall and parade grounds are stone; the natatorium and athletic grounds are to a great extent grass; the auditorium and formal entrances use light; the mosque and students' courtyard use water; the water tower and training areas are sand; and the library and parking court are wood. In the library and parking court, a natural hypostyle of 106 royal palm trees form an oasis with a continuous green canopy leading from the main entrance to the library to frame the procession.

The design explores the range and contrast between harshly amplified conditions of climate and light, and subtly refined sensuous control of these forces within a rigorous organization.

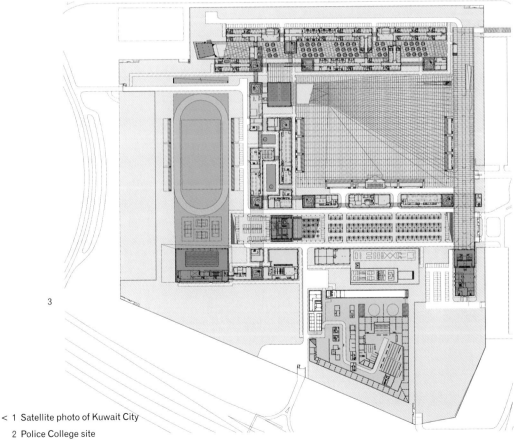

3

< 1 Satellite photo of Kuwait City
  2 Police College site
  3 Color-coded plan of new campus

2

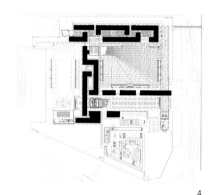

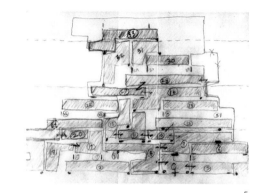

4

5

6

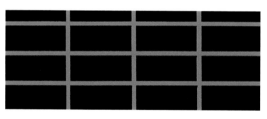

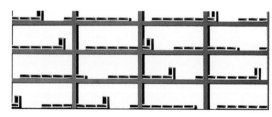

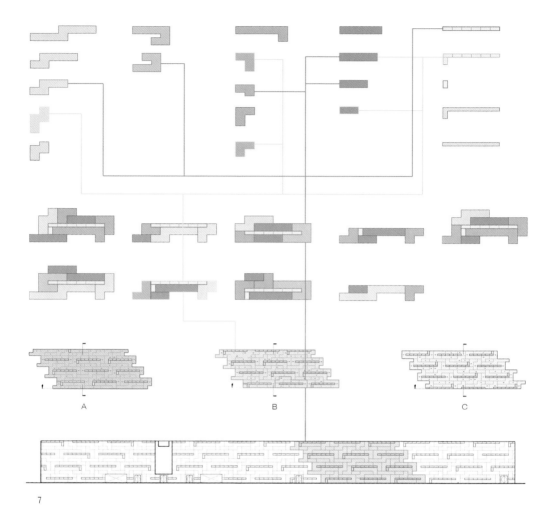

7

4 Location plan of rope buildings
5 Precast wall construction diagram
   showing panel bearing points (two
   minimum) and erection sequence
   required for the topmost panel
6 Rope building interior courtyard.
   Corridor light is shown in color.

7 Precast "puzzle" components: panel
   and window shapes S, C, L, and I; panel
   modules; wall modules; completed wall
8 Precast "puzzle" construction
   sequence: concrete frame;
   CMU infill and steel window frames;
   precast panels; completed wall

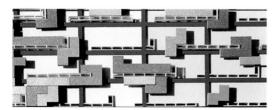
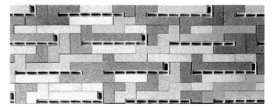

8

9 Academic building corridor with
   Wall Type C: "Illuminated Path"
10 Rope building windows with
   corridor light
11 Rope building exterior wall
   sections.
   Type A: "Illuminated Ceiling";
   Type B: "Observation";
   Type C: "Illuminated Path."
12 Rope building part plans with
   corridor light in local color

10

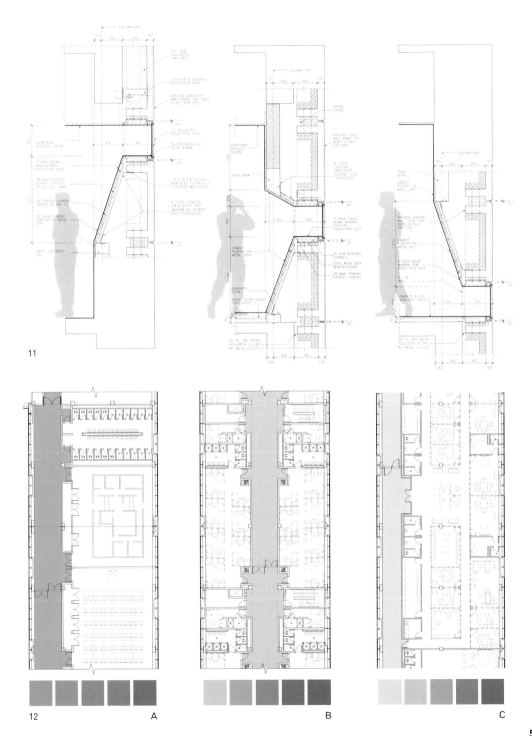

11

12   A   B   C

13

13 Location plan of light chambers
14 Section through horizontal light chamber (bridge)
15 Horizontal light chamber
16 Light chamber plans and computer renderings.
    Chamber names: 1: Sky-Pond; 2: Aperture-Square; 3: Eclipse;
    4: Void-Circle; 5: Slit-Scan; 6: Big Screen; 7: Sculptural;
    8: Big Mac; 9: Untitled; 10: Big Open.

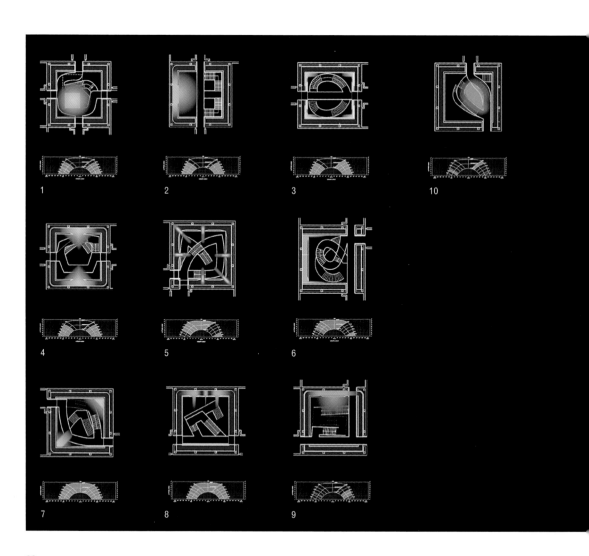

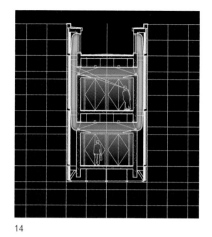

14

15

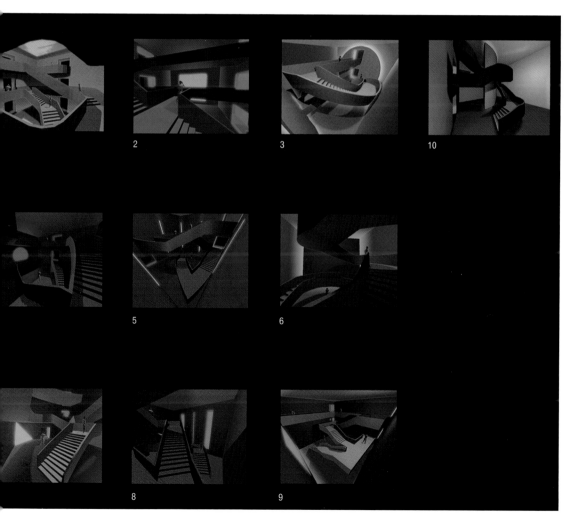

2 3 10

5 6

8 9

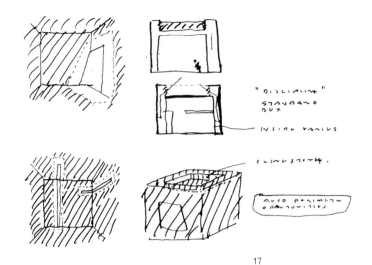

"DISCLAIMR"
STANDARD
BOX

INSIDE VARIES

CLEARSTORY.

AVID PERIMETR
O PAV JUN JILS

17 Concept sketches for light chamber 6
18 Light chamber 6: Big Screen
19 Process drawings of light chamber 6
with James Turrell's comments
20 beige = water tower and sand space

17

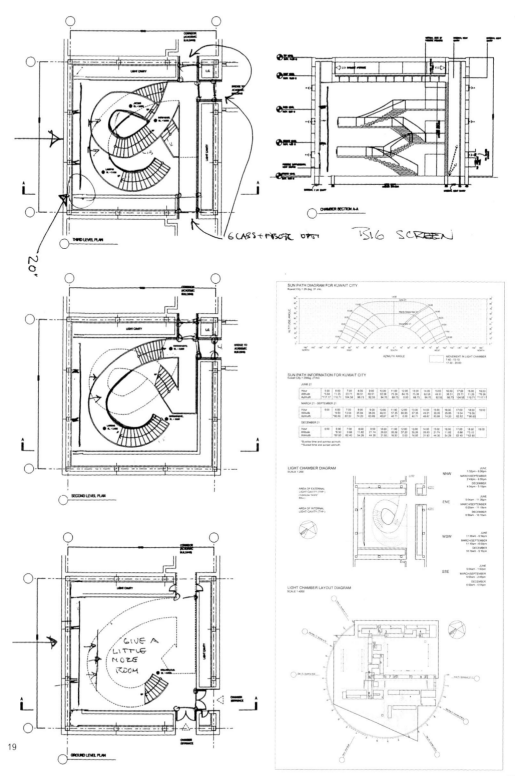

6 CLASS + FIBER OPT

BIG SCREEN

20°

GIVE A
LITTLE
MORE
ROOM

19

20

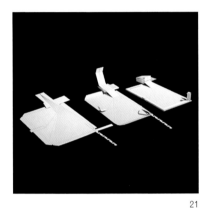

21

22

20 Location plan of vessel buildings and vessel spaces:

green = natatorium and grass space;

blue = mosque and water space;

brown = library and wood space;

gray = dining and stone space;

warm white = auditorium and light space.

21 Folding model of dining hall and stone space
showing material and surface continuity.
Unfolded, mid-fold, and folded.

22 Concept sketches

23 Dining hall and stone (training) space.
Primary materials and lighting are shown in color.

24 Vessel-cube diagram. Each vessel building is
comprised of fragments that together form a
single volume. The joints between fragments are
seams of light.

25 Plan and section of dining hall and stone space.
Primary material is shown in color.

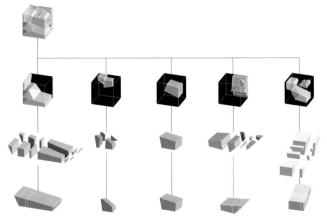

24

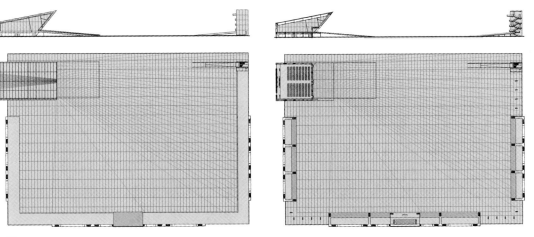

25

26

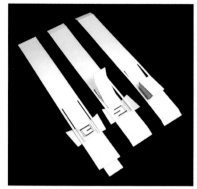

27

26 Model photograph of library interior
27 Folding model of library and wood space
   showing material and surface continuity.
   Unfolded, mid-fold, and folded.
28 Library and wood space. Primary materials
   and lighting are shown in color.
29 Plans, section, and elevation of library and
   wood space. Primary material is shown in color.

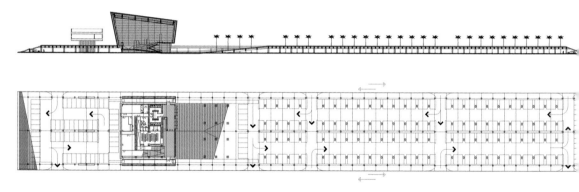

8

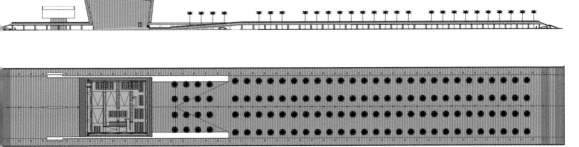

9

30

31

30 Model photograph of mosque at night
31 Folding model of mosque and water space
showing material and surface continuity.
Unfolded, mid-fold, and folded.
32 Mosque and water space. Water and
lighting are shown in color.
33 Plans, section, and elevation of mosque
and water space, water is shown in color.
> 34 Overview of Police College campus

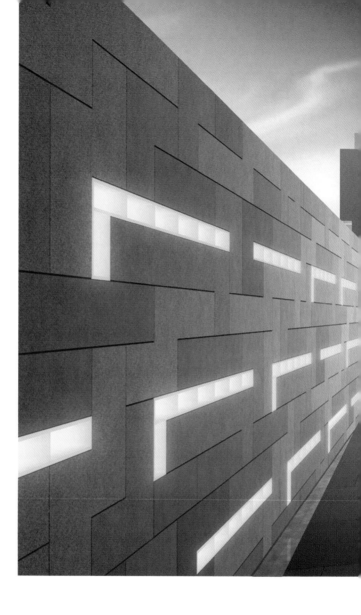

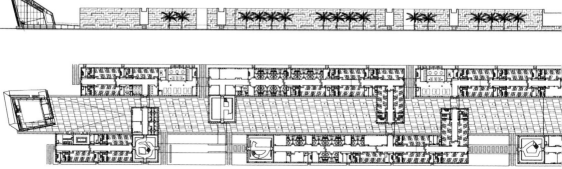

2

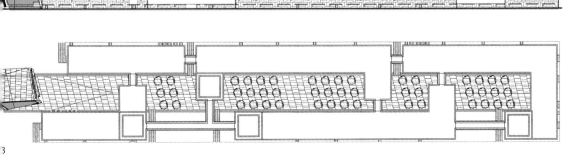

3

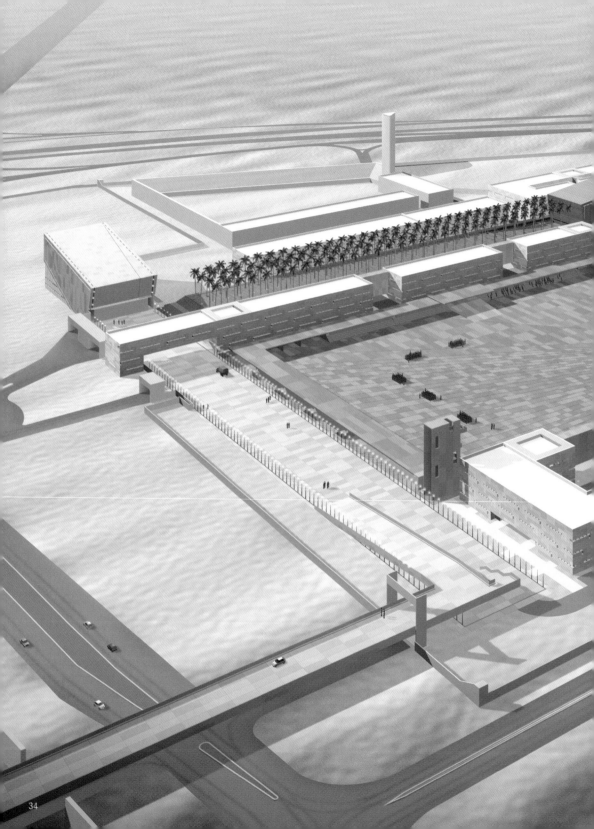

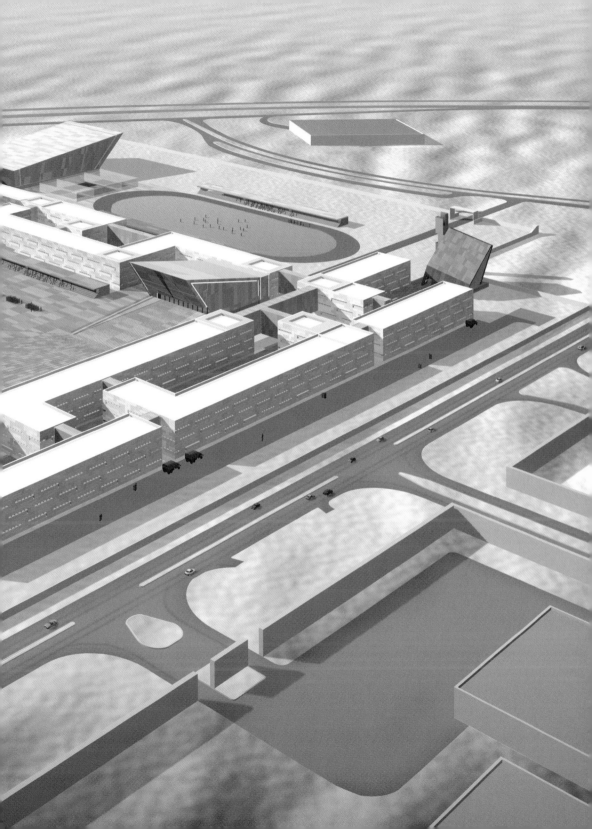

Office Building, 350 Madison Avenue

New York, New York

Designed 1999–2000

Built in 1924, 350 Madison Avenue is an undistinguished brick building located one block from Grand Central Terminal. It has two stories of retail at the base and twenty-four floors of office above. The lobby is in a 25-foot-wide gap between the building proper to the north and another office building to the south. The owner of 350 saw an opportunity to expand the tower by over 50,000 square feet by purchasing air rights from Grand Central Station. Using the unique entrance condition and the prospect of new high-value space at its top, the design attempts to transform the overall impression of the building.

The 350 Madison project is defined by three new elements: a lobby with a glass ceiling that takes advantage of being open to the sky, a volume of new office space at the top of the building clad in floor-to-ceiling glass that affords exceptional views, and a metal and glass curtain wall that partially clads both the new and old elements, linking the two into a single composition.

The new lobby is conceived as a minimal threshold to the office building. A luminous glass floor suspended above the basement level emphatically defines the break between office and street. High-output light fixtures below the floor allow it to glow by day. By night the lobby and the twenty-story space above it are illuminated. This volume of light reverses the current reading of the building entrance as a dark gap in the city fabric.

The new upper levels of the tower formally echo the lobby and are clad in glass panels with minimal joints. The cantilever of the addition allows for larger, more flexible floor plates than the typical floors of the building and opens up dramatic views of mid-town landmarks. The cantilever also facilitates a visual link between the top and bottom that is normally obscured in Manhattan.

A new plane of metal and glass binds the upper and lower elements with the masonry body of the building. Originally conceived as a metal mesh screen, this wall has been designed to enclose new space, overclad an existing wall, act as a roof, and function as a cantilevered soffit. The irregular pattern of panels that make up this surface give it an overall unity while allowing the existing windows and mechanical vents in the masonry building to remain unobstructed. The ceramic frit-coated glass, metal, and corrugated panels were detailed to catch sunlight by day and artificial light, projected up from the lobby, by night.

In recent years there have been many re-claddings of aging New York office buildings. New surfaces smooth over existing masses for an updated appearance. The design of this renovation holds out the possibility of a hybrid construction, where new elements are juxtaposed with the old for a greater effect.

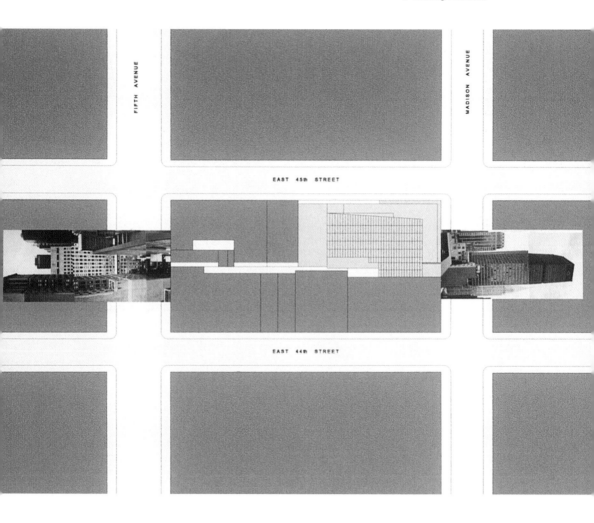

FIFTH AVENUE

MADISON AVENUE

EAST 45th STREET

EAST 44th STREET

4

4 Program diagram

5 Ground floor plan

6 Study models

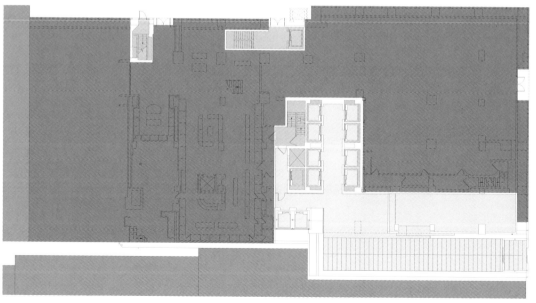

5

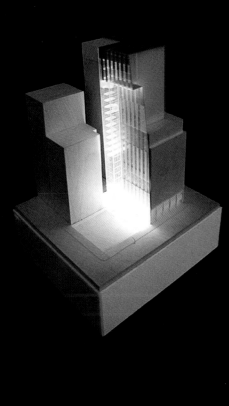

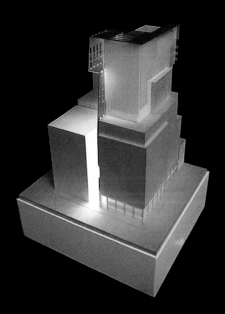

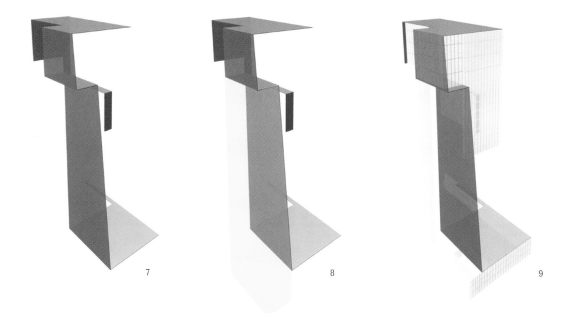

7 Metal panel diagram
8 Metal panel with trapped volume
9 Metal panel with curtain wall
10 Concept model
11 Existing south elevation
12 South elevation with metal panel façade
13 Façade detail

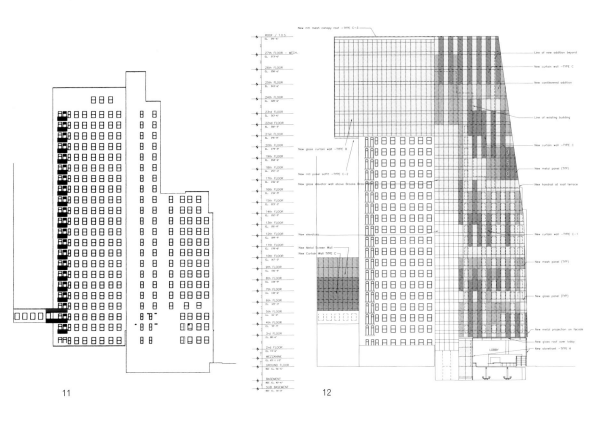

11

12

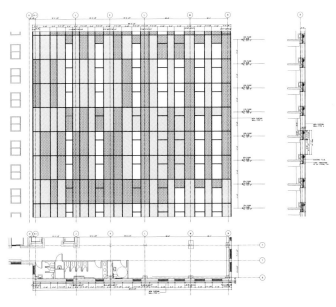

13

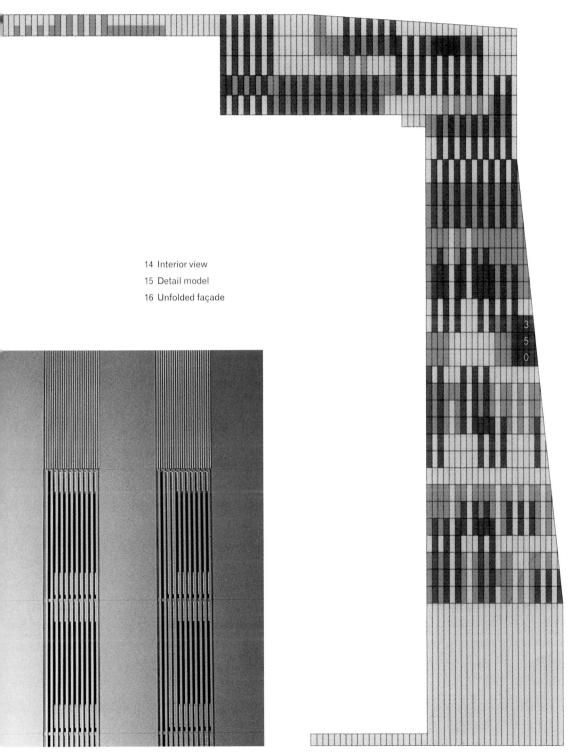

14 Interior view
15 Detail model
16 Unfolded façade

16

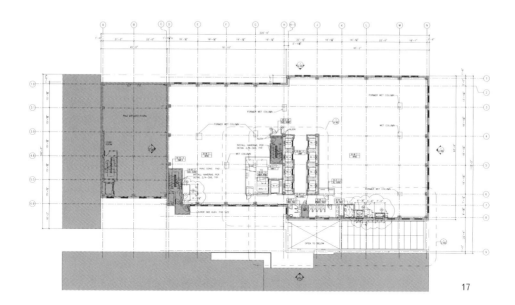

17

18

17 Typical floor plan

18 Rendered view from Madison Avenue

19 View from Madison Avenue

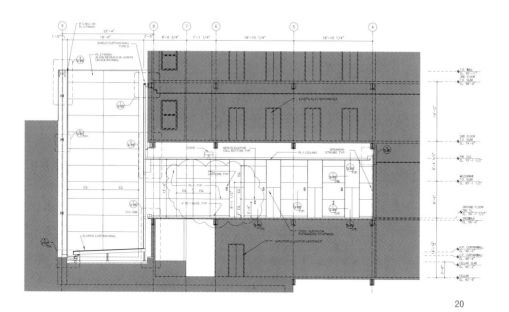

20

21

20 Section facing south

21 Interior view

22 Rendered interior view of lobby

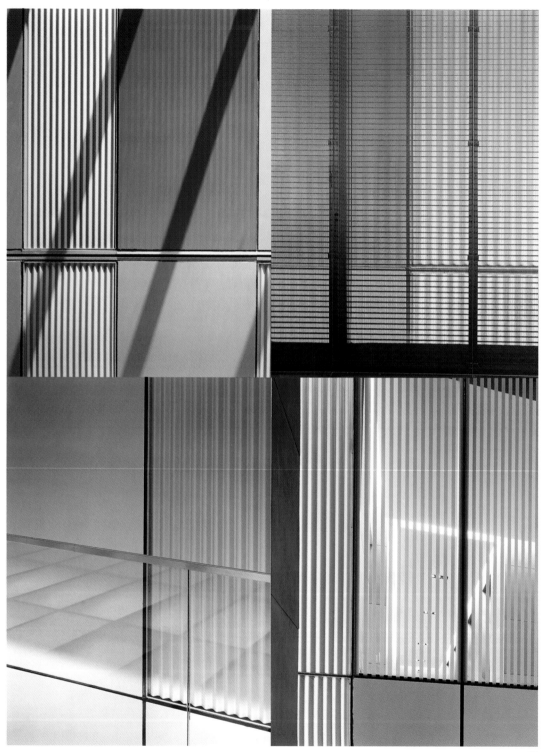

24

Bank Headquarters, Marina Bay

Singapore

Designed 2000–01

The island of Singapore has been enlarged by 10 percent since 1967 at the expense of its topography. A large undeveloped tract of real estate formed by landfill is adjacent to the city financial center and surrounds a body of water known as Marina Bay. The Urban Development Authority (URA) of Singapore has created a master plan for the area that projects a volume and density of construction that would dwarf the existing downtown. One parcel of the landfill measuring 37,000 square meters that faces Marina Bay and downtown Singapore is the site for this project.

The site is planned for 400,000 square meters of development. Of this space 70 percent is programmed for office use, 20 percent for serviced apartments, and the remainder for restaurants, retail, entertainment, and other amenities that serve the building tenants. A parking garage will fill the footprint of the site on two levels below grade. Although the Singapore skyline features many office towers of fifty or more floors, a height limit of thirty stories has been imposed on this site.

The URA Master Plan envisions a group of several thirty-story buildings on the site. The bank program, however, requires some very large floor plates of 6,000 to 8,000 square meters and connections between floors to allow better interdepartmental communication and circulation. This yields a plan with a row of service cores joined periodically by large floors. The gaps that occur between floors of conventional dimensions have been programmed as gardens featuring amenities ordinarily found only at ground level. Since the links between the cores are to be column free, a system of steel trusses three stories deep that span about 70 meters has been developed. This structure brings load to the ground efficiently and, in addition, allows the building section to be discontinuous because the trusses carry groups of three floors independently. A result of the flexible section is office floors with varied lease depths that will accommodate the variety of office layouts demanded today and can be changed over time to accommodate new plan configurations. The curved slab of the office building, derived from

2

the demands of the building program, is sited at the edge of Marina Bay. Viewed from downtown, it has a monumental presence because of its unity, yet its rippled elevation with large garden terraces has a scale appropriate to the neighborhood. To provide a column-free office perimeter and to avoid the corrosiveness of the humid marine environment, the steel truss structure occupies a meter-wide void space created by the layers of a double-skin curtain wall. Fitted with clear glass, the double-skin façade improves the energy efficiency of the building by creating a buffer zone of circulating air that is between the temperature of the interior and the exterior. Behind the office slab is a seven-story structure that provides a transition to a planned smaller scale residential neighborhood. The building is comprised of a similar vocabulary of components as the office, but their orientation is rotated ninety degrees to correspond to the site. The open terraces in the slab reappear as courtyards in the low building to allow daylight into the center of the block. The undulations of the Marina Bay façade are seen again in the form of the topography that defines the character of the seventh-level roof.

The form of this office project reflects influences that are both internal and external. The plan and section have curved, irregular profiles that provide planning flexibility while echoing the play of light reflected off the bay. The openings in the office slab create spaces for interaction demanded by the program while creating framed views through the building. It is hoped that by imbedding exciting public spaces high in the section of the office block integrated with residential units the monotony of a conventional stratified development will be overcome.

< 1 Evolution of the office from the 15th
         century to the present
< 2 View of site across Marina Bay showing
         relationship to existing downtown
   3 Site model
   4 Plan view with expanded downtown
> 5 Land-side view

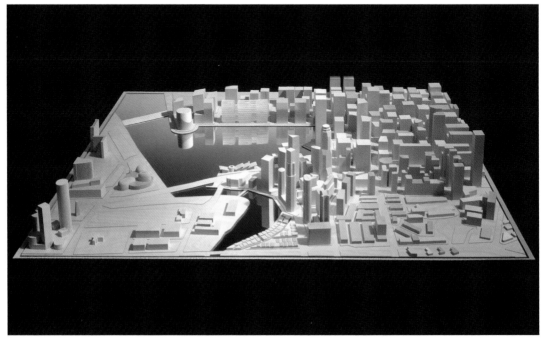

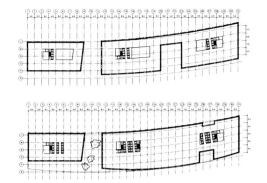
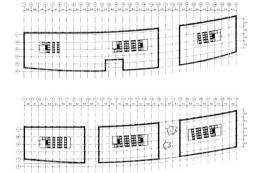

6

7

6 Typical floor plans

7 Sectional perspective

8 Ground floor plan

9 Garden and open space

10 Serviced apartments

11 Vehicular circulation

12 Office and trading

13 Pedestrian circulation

14 Retail use

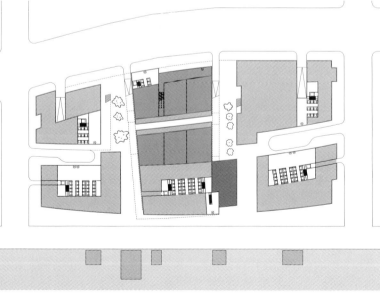

8

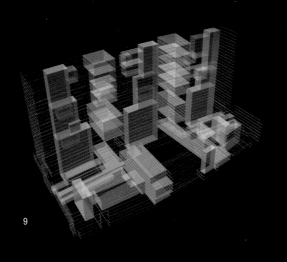

9

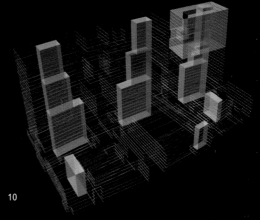

10

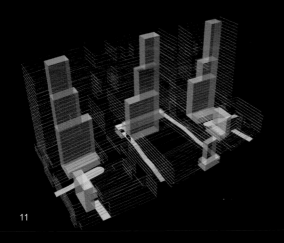

11

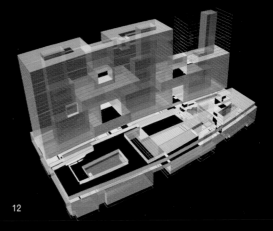

12

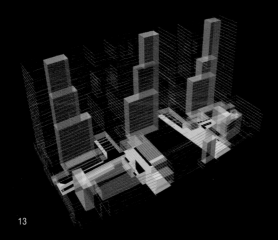

13

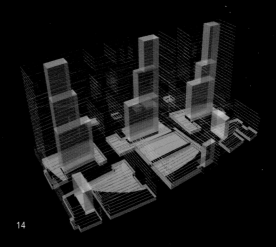

14

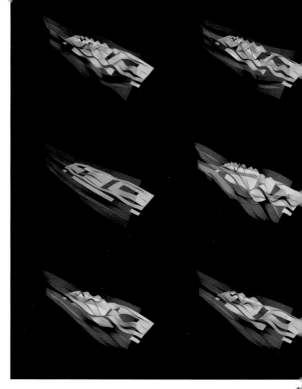

15

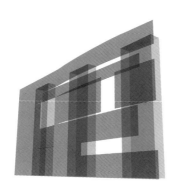

17

15 Urban infrastructure diagram
16 Frequency and amplitude studies
17 Frame study
18 Massing study
19 Surface study
20 Volume study

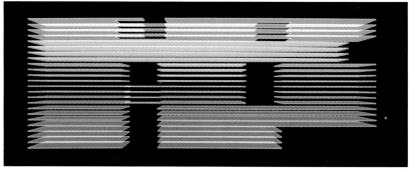

18

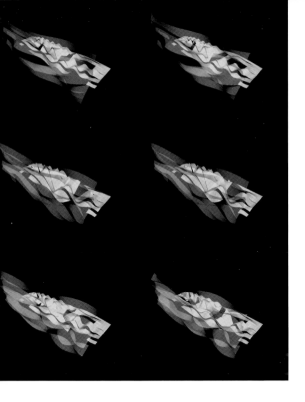

19

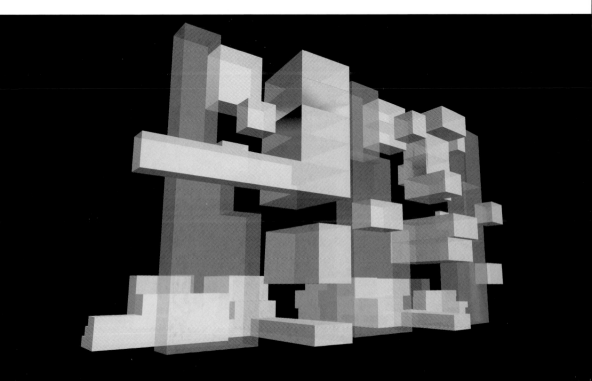

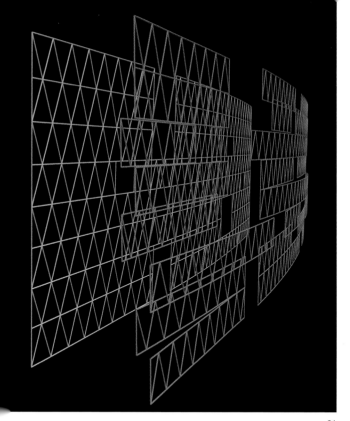

21

22

23

21 Structural diagram
22 Façade detail with exposed
   steel truss
23 Model detail showing
   undulating trusses
24 Massing study
25 Model in context
26 View through elevated garden
   to downtown
27 Elevation from Marina Bay
28 North-south section through
   trading
29 North-south section through
   gardens

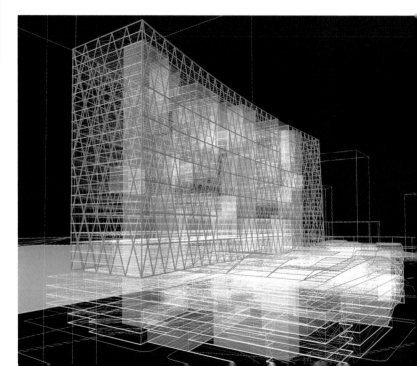

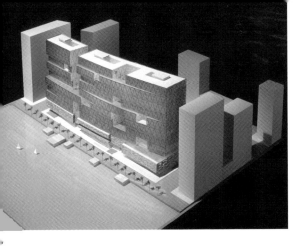

26

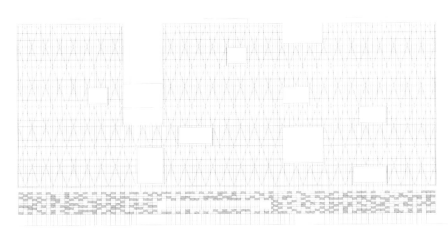

27

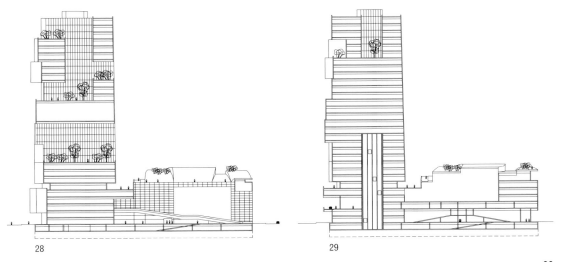

28

29

30

31

32

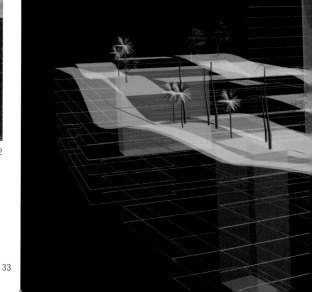

33

34

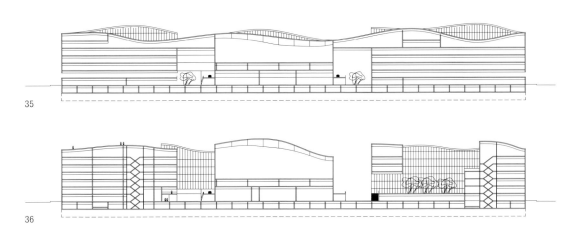

35

36

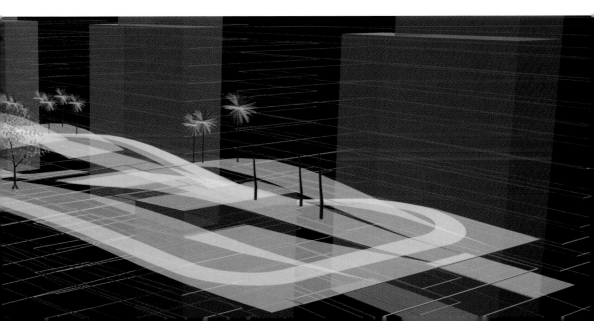

Terminal 3 Building, Changi International Airport

Singapore

Designed 2000–01

Changi is one of the world's top-rated international airports. The terminal complex was planned in successive phases to be built in response to demand. The first, built in 1981, is located on axis with the tree-lined boulevard that links the airport with downtown Singapore. The second, built in 1991, is adjacent to it and is oriented parallel to the roadway. Construction has begun on Terminal 3, and it mirrors the massing of Terminal 2 across the boulevard. The airport functions as a transfer hub for long-distance flights and therefore offers an exceptional array of amenities such as swimming pools, gardens, and movie theaters (as well as the usual retail and food service establishments) for passengers with long layovers. Singapore's airport authority wanted the appearance of the new terminal to be harmonious with that of the existing buildings while responding to the airport program and the tropical climate in a unique way.

The major spaces of the terminal are organized in a series of functional zones 300 meters long that are layered from east to west. At the front of the terminal, adjacent to the departures curb, is a 15-meter-wide band devoted to vertical circulation and landscaping. The ticketing hall occupies the next zone, which is bounded by columns 60 meters apart. A continuous 30-meter-wide opening in the departure hall floor, interrupted only by bridges, defines a second band of landscaping planted between the claim devices in the arrival hall. The last zone of the terminal is occupied by a multilevel departure lounge with retail, concessions, and other amenities. Each of the airport's functional zones has specific light-

ing requirements. The ticketing area requires uniform, glare-free light for optimal legibility of signage and flight information on plasma screen displays. The heavily landscaped zones require natural daylight at high levels of illumination. Circulation and retail requirements are less strictly defined and offer the opportunity for variation in the pattern and intensity of light.

A single flat roof spans the major spaces of the terminal. At 250 meters by 300 meters it covers approximately 22 acres. Cable-braced steel trusses 250 meters long, 4 meters deep, and spaced 15 meters apart allow the roof to extend over the multiple zones of the terminal including a 60-meter-wide clear span in the ticketing hall and a 20-meter-wide cantilever over the departures road. Within the structural framework of the roof a pattern of two thousand skylight openings has been established that will allow the terminal to be illuminated completely by natural daylight for eight hours a day, regardless of cloud cover. The skylights are of a uniform 2.5-by-5-meter dimension that allows for precise repetitive construction similar to a curtain wall. Daylight is modified by a system of louvers both above and below the roof to meet the requirements of the zones of the building. The perforated aluminum external louvers are part of a continuous secondary roof system that shades and protects the primary roof membrane. Supported by the skylight curbs, these louvers are adjusted by motors controlled by a computerized system that measures incoming daylight. On cloudy days they open to admit the maximum amount of illumination. If the sensors detect a cloudless sky, the louvers close to limit the amount of light and heat entering the building. In landscaped areas, the louvers are designed to reflect additional daylight towards the plants. More light is also allowed into the circulation and retail areas where changing patterns on the floor and walls help animate the space.

The system of louvers below the roof is supported by slender high-tension steel cables which are secured to the bottom of the trusses. These louvers are fixed at specific angles that allow some to channel daylight to the floor of the terminal while others reflect light up to the ceiling which would otherwise be dark in contrast to the skylights. By night, artificial light from easily accessible sources near the floor is reflected off the louvers to provide uniform illumination within the terminal.

Although the components of the roof system have been arrayed to fulfill specific technical requirements in the various zones of the building, their overall appearance is intended to be homogeneous. The large number of angled metal surfaces blur the legibility of the structural truss, skylight openings, and ceiling plane to soften their otherwise technical quality. As passengers move beneath the ceiling, shifting relationships between the panels add to the sense of dynamism in the terminal.

1 Aerial view of Changi Airport
2 Airport plan

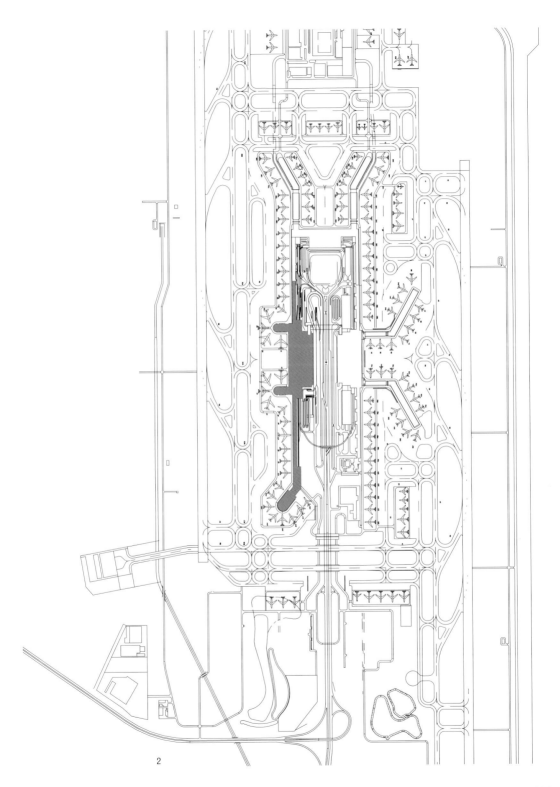

2

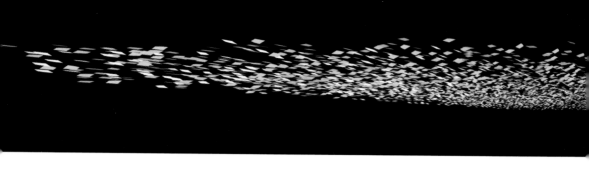

3 Louver field concept drawing

4 Aerial view of new terminal

5 Concept model of roof

6 Overall model of terminal

7 Structural diagram

4

5

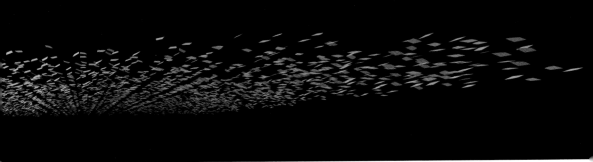

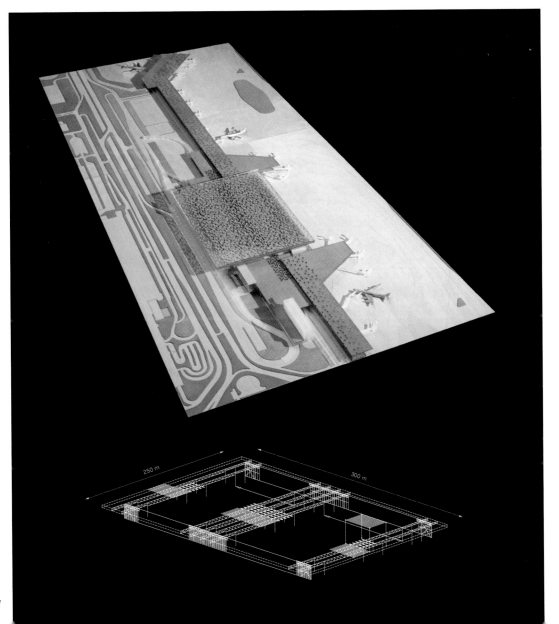

250 m

300 m

8, 9, 10

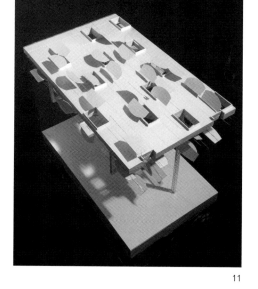

11

12

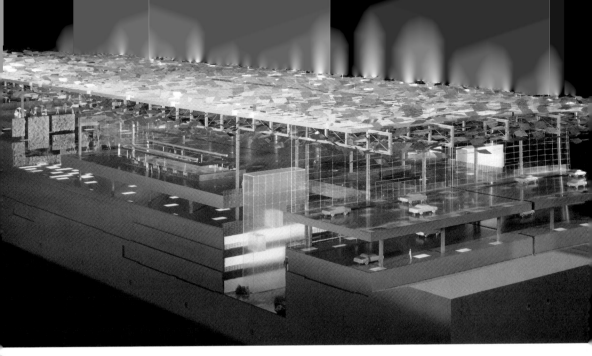

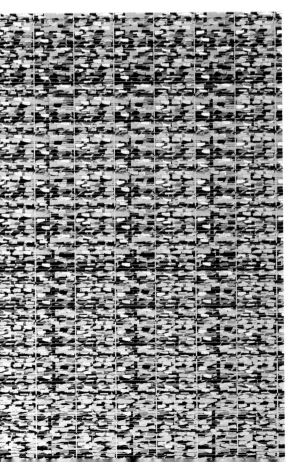

14

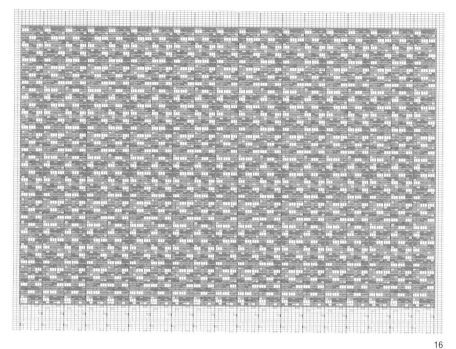

16

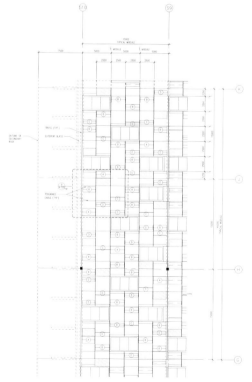

17

16 Overall ceiling plan

17 Plan detail of ceiling

18 Rendered view of ceiling

19 Rendered view of curbside

20 Exploded view of roof components

21–23 Louver support details

19

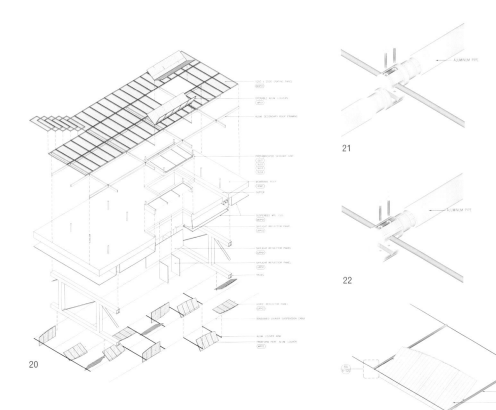

20

21

22

23

ALUMINUM PIPE

ALUMINUM PIPE

PANEL SUPPORT ELEMENT

MCP23

SUSPENSION CABLE

113

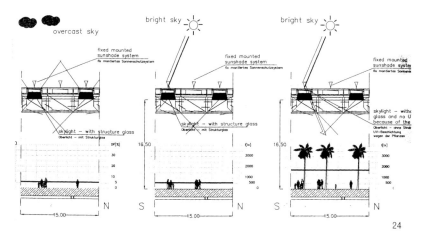

overcast sky
bright sky
bright sky

fixed mounted sunshade system
fix montiertes Sonnenschutzsystem

skylight – with structure glass
Oberlicht – mit Strukturglas

skylight – with structure glass
Oberlicht – mit Strukturglas

skylight – without glass and no UV because of the
Oberlicht – ohne Struktur UV-Beschichtung wegen der Pflanzen

24

25

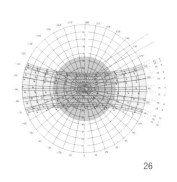

26

27

28

29

30

31

32

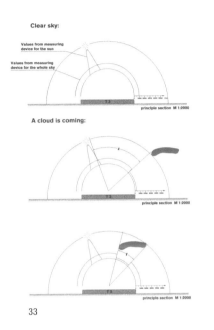

Clear sky:

Values from measuring
device for the sun

Values from measuring
device for the whole sky

principle section M 1:2000

A cloud is coming:

principle section M 1:2000

principle section M 1:2000

33

34

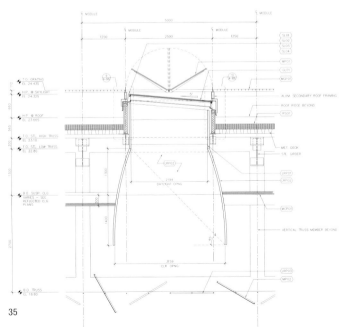

35

24 Mechanized louver operation
     diagrams
25 Artificial sky testing laboratory
26 Singapore solar data
27–32 Test model under artificial sky
33 Cloud sensor diagram
34 Model of operable louver
35 Detail of skylight and louver
     system

36

37

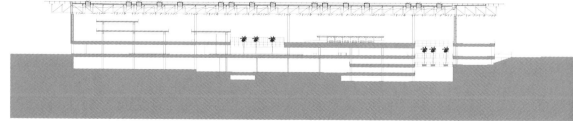

38

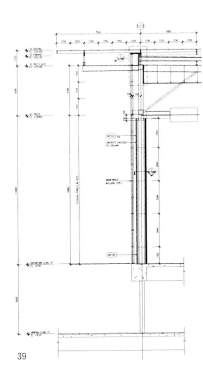

39

36 Rendered view of roof cantilever

37 Rendered view at SMRT station interface

38 Section

39 Detail section at cantilever

40 Aerial view of final scheme with operable louvers

> 41 Interior view of final scheme

40

Case Studies: Glass and Steel Structural Systems

These four projects illustrate an effort by a team of architects and engineers to develop building enclosure systems that employ steel and glass in innovative ways. All of the studies have involved research into new manufacturing and construction techniques that could yield unexpected results when seen in the built work.

The Jubilee Pavilion is an entrance to an underground retail arcade in a London park. It is intended to have a quiet presence in the landscape, achieved by transparency. The exclusive use of glass for all surfaces of the enclosure also maximizes the amount of daylight reaching the several underground levels of the project. Unique systems employed include a glass-ballasted catenary roof and glass rod downspouts.

The People Mover Station is in downtown Detroit. Here a glass envelope encircles the platforms of the station and the rail cars themselves. A system of colored glass panels screens daylight and provides a weather enclosure while allowing for natural ventilation. A new process will be used to fabricate the laminated, colored, etched glass panels.

The GM Headquarters Lobby is an interior renovation. Here a curtain of glass defines a new circulation path within an existing space. The minimal detailing of the steel system that suspends the glass scrim allows it to read as a surface rather than a cage of structural elements. A new type of locked cable has been employed in the structure.

The GM Gallery employs elements similar to those in the lobby, however their horizontal orientation defines the ceiling plane. The luminous etched glass surface is given a floating quality by its innovative support system.

2, 3, 4

Glass Support System: Four catenary cables, connected by support masts, suspend a blanket of roof and walls of glass. The shape is defined through responses to the below-grade program, park buildings, and landscape, combined with the natural catenary load-flow force curve. Two draped upper main catenary cables (60 mm) and two lower inverted-curve edge catenary cables (40 mm) are linked to each other by tie-down cables (16 mm). The resulting cable network locates spatial nodes that organize the horizontal and vertical geometry of the glass envelope.

Glass Ballast: Instead of weighting the upper catenary cables for uplift resistance, as in a more traditional concrete approach (Oakland Coliseum), the Jubilee Pavilion explores the use of three 12-millimeter layers of laminated and insulated glass as roof ballast. This structural approach resists galloping uplift while providing visual lightness and pattern layering of the glass sandwich.

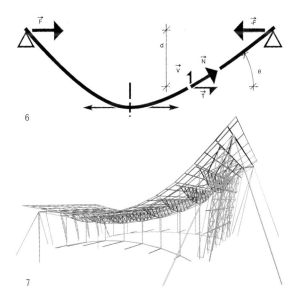

6

7

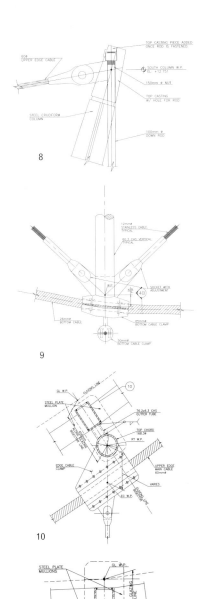

8

9

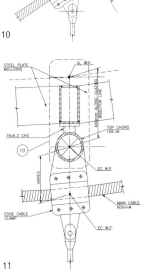

10

11

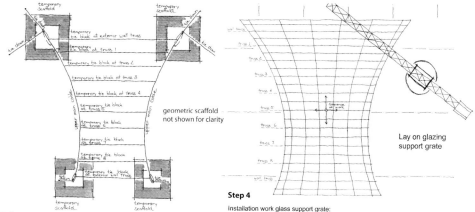

Assembly Step 1

Temporary bracings installed at location of roof trusses to support geometry

Step 4

Installation work glass support grate:

Exactly pre-assembled glass supporting grate delivered to site

Start above truss 5 and installed symmetrically to both sides

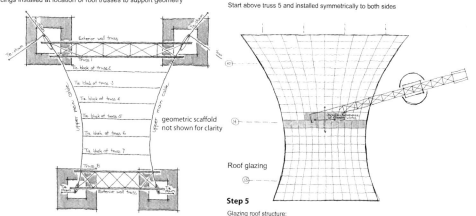

Step 2

Exterior wall truss and adjacent truss pre-assembled and lifted into position

Step 5

Glazing roof structure:

Start above truss 5 and installed symmetrically to both sides

Forces in cables surveyed and adjusted according to advancement of glazing

12

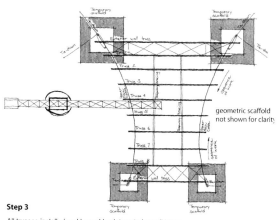

Step 3

All trusses installed and braced back to exterior wall truss

Final roof geometry surveyed against model and adjusted

Additional cables installed into roof structure

12 Glass plank roof assembly

13 Structural model

Glass Plank Roof Assembly: First, four steel and wood pylons are propped with tie-down cables, and upper and lower catenary cables are attached to the pylons. Next, the catenary tie-down cables are attached and partially stressed. Lateral-spanning cable trusses and transverse-stabilizing cables are then placed, establishing the geometry for glazing purlins to follow. Finally, primary and secondary purlin framing is installed. Glass planks are fitted, and final cable stressing is completed.

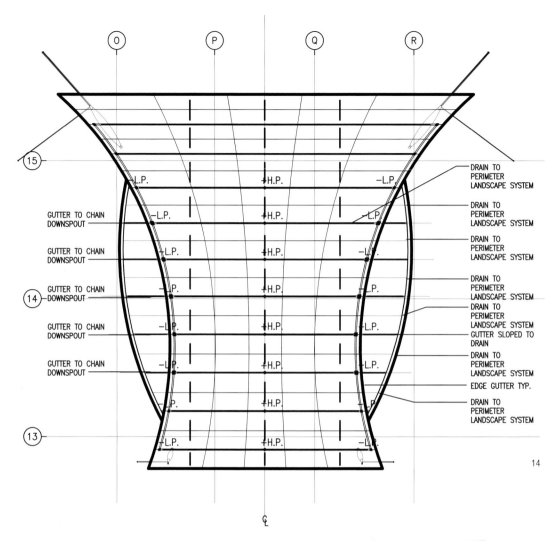

OPQR

15

L.P. +H.P. −L.P.

DRAIN TO PERIMETER LANDSCAPE SYSTEM

GUTTER TO CHAIN DOWNSPOUT
−L.P. +H.P. −L.P.

DRAIN TO PERIMETER LANDSCAPE SYSTEM

GUTTER TO CHAIN DOWNSPOUT
L.P. +H.P. −L.P.

DRAIN TO PERIMETER LANDSCAPE SYSTEM

GUTTER TO CHAIN DOWNSPOUT
14 L.P. +H.P. L.P.

DRAIN TO PERIMETER LANDSCAPE SYSTEM

GUTTER TO CHAIN DOWNSPOUT
−L.P. +H.P. L.P.

DRAIN TO PERIMETER LANDSCAPE SYSTEM
GUTTER SLOPED TO DRAIN

GUTTER TO CHAIN DOWNSPOUT
−L.P. +H.P. L.P.

DRAIN TO PERIMETER LANDSCAPE SYSTEM

EDGE GUTTER TYP.

P. +H.P. P.

DRAIN TO PERIMETER LANDSCAPE SYSTEM

13 L.P. +H.P. −L.P.

14

Ç

Glass Water Mitigation: Upper and lower catenary glass roofs utilize transversely sloped gutter systems that ride atop lateral trussing as hidden slots between glass panels. Water is directed from a centralized high point to low points at the edges. Sixty-millimeter glass rod "downspouts" transfer water from upper to lower gutters.

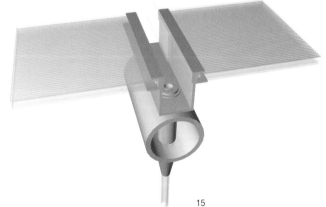

15

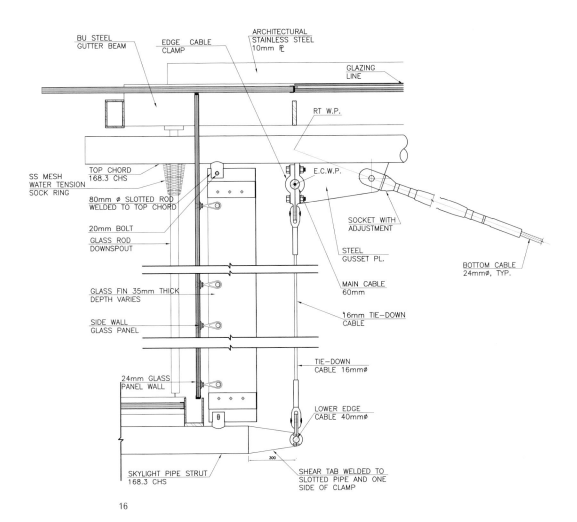

BU STEEL
GUTTER BEAM

EDGE CABLE
CLAMP

ARCHITECTURAL
STAINLESS STEEL
10mm ℞

GLAZING
LINE

RT W.P.

SS MESH
WATER TENSION
SOCK RING

TOP CHORD
168.3 CHS

E.C.W.P.

80mm ∅ SLOTTED ROD
WELDED TO TOP CHORD

20mm BOLT

GLASS ROD
DOWNSPOUT

SOCKET WITH
ADJUSTMENT

STEEL
GUSSET PL.

BOTTOM CABLE
24mm∅, TYP.

GLASS FIN 35mm THICK
DEPTH VARIES

MAIN CABLE
60mm

SIDE WALL
GLASS PANEL

16mm TIE-DOWN
CABLE

24mm GLASS
PANEL WALL

TIE-DOWN
CABLE 16mm∅

LOWER EDGE
CABLE 40mm∅

SKYLIGHT PIPE STRUT
168.3 CHS

300

SHEAR TAB WELDED TO
SLOTTED PIPE AND ONE
SIDE OF CLAMP

16

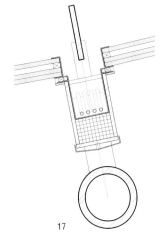

17

Support System: A six-column cantilevered painted steel truss superstructure, utilizing diagonal and vertical steel channel secondary framing, links the mainframe to the glazing bracket arms. Stainless steel bracket arms and glazing channel clips orient and connect inverted vertical glass panels to the secondary vertical channels. The primary shape is defined by platform length regulations, vertical transportation requirements, limited air rights for column-bearing points to existing multilevel below-grade basements, and the design intention to visually and physically lift the building from the ground, thus permitting park continuity. The secondary shape orients the circulation and the views into and out of the station through the implementation of laminated, colored etched glass on the northern and southern elevations and clear, vision glass on the eastern and western elevations.

Glass Shingles: Working with a program requirement to naturally ventilate the station for energy and maintenance savings, the broad northern and southern elevations of laminated, colored etched glass are rotated in a lapped, shingled manner, permitting natural ventilation, filtering sunlight, and shedding rainwater. Similarly, internal night-lighting of the shingles creates paired planes of stained glass, embracing arriving and departing visitors inside and outside the building. Vertical panels of clear glass at the east and west stairway façades provide long-distance park vistas and visual security from the street.

Glass Brackets: A series of 12-inch stainless steel channel clips attached to 3/4-by-2-inch stainless steel bar arms seats and holds each typical 36-by-87-inch shingle and vertical glass panel. The repetition of glazing assembly envelops the entire station with cantilevered glass end panels, accentuating the cantilevered superstructure truss within.

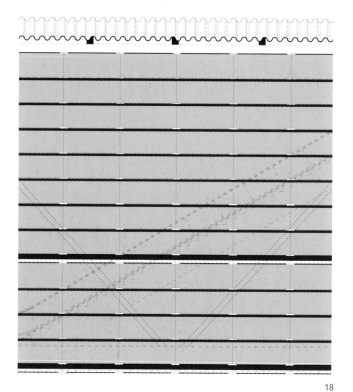

18

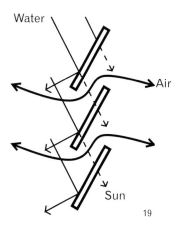

Water

Air

Sun

19

18 Partial elevation

19 Section diagram

20 Wire frame diagram

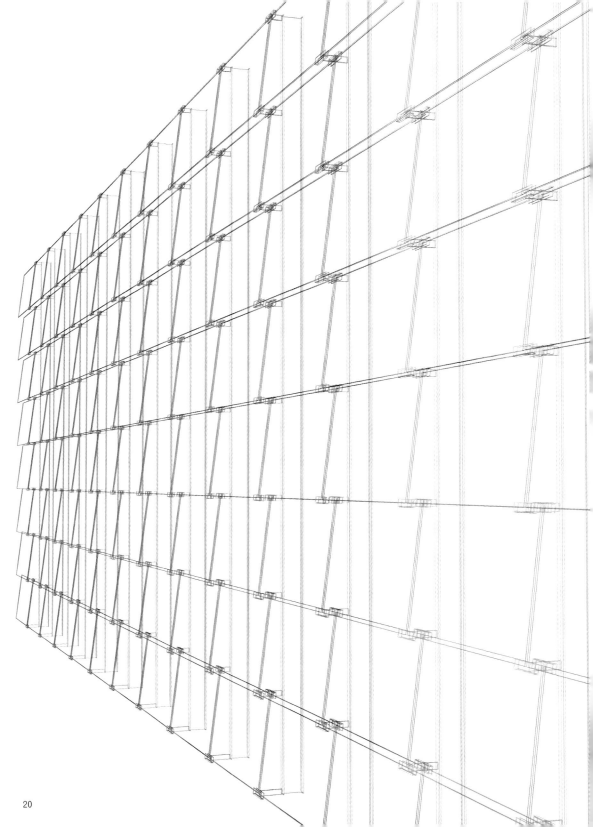

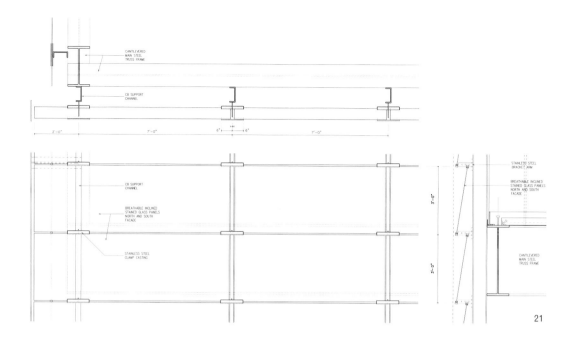

CANTILEVERED
MAIN STEEL
TRUSS FRAME

C8 SUPPORT
CHANNEL

C8 SUPPORT
CHANNEL

BREATHABLE INCLINED
STAINED GLASS PANELS
NORTH AND SOUTH
FACADE

STAINLESS STEEL
CLAMP CASTING

STAINLESS STEEL
BRACKET ARM

BREATHABLE INCLINED
STAINED GLASS PANELS
NORTH AND SOUTH
FACADE

CANTILEVERED
MAIN STEEL
TRUSS FRAME

21

21 Typical bay of glass shingle wall

22 Section of glass connection

23 View of glass shingle wall

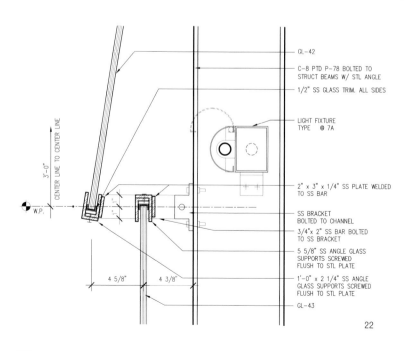

GL-42

C-8 PTD P-78 BOLTED TO
STRUCT BEAMS W/ STL ANGLE

1/2" SS GLASS TRIM. ALL SIDES

LIGHT FIXTURE
TYPE @ 7A

2" x 3" x 1/4" SS PLATE WELDED
TO SS BAR

SS BRACKET
BOLTED TO CHANNEL

3/4"x 2" SS BAR BOLTED
TO SS BRACKET

5 5/8" SS ANGLE GLASS
SUPPORTS SCREWED
FLUSH TO STL PLATE

1'-0" x 2 1/4" SS ANGLE
GLASS SUPPORTS SCREWED
FLUSH TO STL PLATE

GL-43

CENTER LINE TO CENTER LINE
3'-0"

W.P.

4 5/8"   4 3/8"

22

Glass Support System: This system consists of discrete 1/2-inch locked suspension cables with stainless steel glass bracket clamps. The shape of the lobby's glass wall and gallery hall's glass ceiling as well as the use and organization of that material intend to redefine the scale, clarify the path, and visually layer the adjacent program within an existing multiuse facility. Through the use of contrasting but complementary materials of suspended, rear-illuminated glass and stainless steel in the intervention of the 30-foot-high glass lobby wall and 200-foot-long glass gallery hall ceiling, ideas of new occupancy and way-finding clarity within a 600-square-foot existing complex are explored.

Glass Lamination and Layering: The typical vertical lobby wall unit is comprised of three 100-by-54-inch laminated, colored etched glass panels which are suspended end to end vertically. The juxtaposition of these three-tiered units in a twenty-unit curvilinear array redefines the lobby's spatial boundary, circulation, and tonal layer patterns of color translucency.

Glass Rear-Illumination: Ceiling combinations of spot and flood lighting with low-voltage cable clip accent lamps further develop daytime and nighttime tonal layering and definition of the lobby's glass wall. Similarly, florescent lighting units provide rhythm and continuity to the gallery hall's glass ceiling.

24

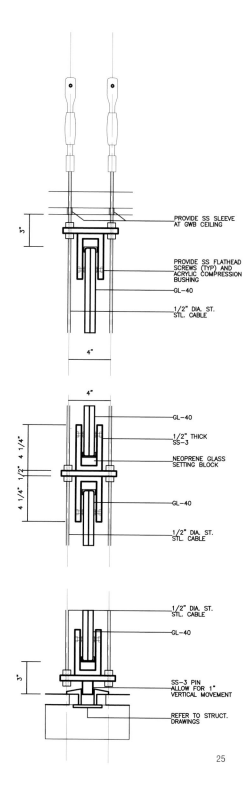

PROVIDE SS SLEEVE AT GWB CEILING

PROVIDE SS FLATHEAD SCREWS (TYP) AND ACRYLIC COMPRESSION BUSHING

GL–40

1/2" DIA. ST. STL. CABLE

4"

4"

GL–40

1/2" THICK SS–3

NEOPRENE GLASS SETTING BLOCK

GL–40

1/2" DIA. ST. STL. CABLE

1/2" DIA. ST. STL. CABLE

GL–40

SS–3 PIN ALLOW FOR 1" VERTICAL MOVEMENT

REFER TO STRUCT. DRAWINGS

25

26

24 Plan
25 Section
26 View of typical glass connection
27 Locked cable

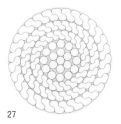

27

Similar to the sandwich composition of the lobby wall, the gallery hall ceiling employs laminated, colored etched glass. Quarter-inch wound cables suspend each frameless glass panel below the existing ceiling, minimizing attachment shadow and providing a new continuously illuminated path from the lobby to the office-level circulator ring beyond. The typical ceiling units of the gallery hall are comprised of 3-by-12-foot laminated, colored etched glass panels. Access for adjustment, maintenance, and lighting replacement is provided from the sides and facilitated by removable cable clamp fittings.

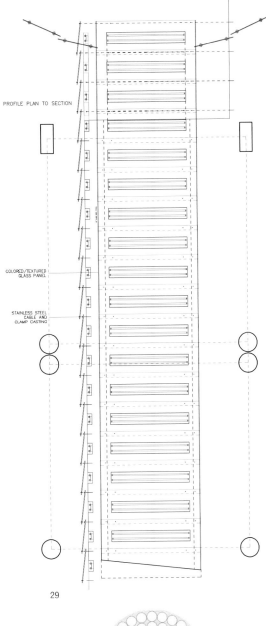

PROFILE PLAN TO SECTION

COLORED/TEXTURED
GLASS PANEL

STAINLESS STEEL
CABLE AND
CLAMP CASTING

29

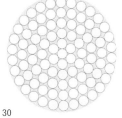

30

28 View of typical glass connection

29 Section and reflected plan

30 Wound cable

Walter Netsch Interviewed by Detlef Mertins

May 21, 2001

1700 North Hudson Street, Chicago

Walter Netsch was born on February 23, 1920 in Chicago and studied architecture at the Massachusetts Institute of Technology, graduating in 1943. After several years of service in the U.S. Army Corps of Engineers, he worked with the architect L. Morgan Yost in 1946–47 and then joined Skidmore, Owings & Merrill, first in the San Francisco office (1947–51) and then in Chicago (1951–79) where he became partner in 1951. Netsch established a distinctive approach to design using what he called "field theory," a highly versatile approach to the geometric generation of architectonic structures intended to be uniquely suited to their purposes and environments. Netsch's major works include the United States Naval Postgraduate Technical School (Monterey, California, 1952–55), Inland Steel Building (Chicago, Illinois, 1954–58), United States Air Force Academy (Colorado Springs, Colorado, 1956–62), the University of Illinois Science Center and Architecture and Art Laboratories (Chicago, Illinois, both completed 1965), the Library at Wells College (Aurora, New York, 1968), the Regenstein Libraries of Northwestern University (Evanston, Illinois, 1970) and the University of Chicago (Chicago, Illinois, 1961), and the Miami University Art Museum (Miami, Florida, 1979). He has received honorary doctorates from Lawrence University, Miami University, Northwestern University, and Purdue University. His work has been exhibited at the Colorado Springs Art Museum, the Miami University Art Museum, the Museum of Modern Art in New York, and the Museum of Contemporary Art in Chicago. The United States Air Force Academy (1954–62),

which is featured here, involved the construction of buildings with a total area of 2,217,150 square feet in a mesa of the Rocky Mountains, outside of Colorado Springs, Colorado. Its program includes living space for the cadets as well as spaces for academic instruction, library and museum, administration, religious services, recreation, and athletics (both indoor and outdoor). The credits for the project within Skidmore, Owings & Merrill are as follows: Nathaniel A. Owings, Partner, Head of Design and Production Team; John O. Merrill, Partner, Director; Carroll L. Tyler, General Manager; Gordon Bunshaft, Partner in Charge of Design; Walter Netsch, Director of Design; and Jack Train, Director of Production.

Detlef Mertins is Associate Professor at the University of Toronto where he directs the graduate program in architecture. He has written extensively on the history of modernism in the 20th century, including recently published essays in the catalogues for *Mies in Berlin* (Museum of Modern Art) and *Mies in America* (Canadian Center for Architecture and Whitney Museum of American Art). He has also been professional advisor for several design competitions in Canada, including the Downsview Park Competition (Toronto, 1999–2000), which is the subject of a book forthcoming through the Graduate School of Design, Harvard University.

DETLEF MERTINS: The United States Air Force Academy in Colorado Springs has been recognized as one of the most distinguished projects of SOM and,

more broadly, of modern architecture in America. The architects were selected in 1954, and the Academy was opened in 1958. The Chapel was completed in 1962. The project received the American Institute of Architects 25 Year Award in 1982. As a young man, how did you get to work on it, and what was your relationship with Gordon Bunshaft?

WALTER NETSCH: I was given the full responsibility for the design of the Academy. I was thirty-four years of age. Today you have to be fifty, although there are some younger architects coming up too. Of course, Gordon was the chief of design and came to the client meetings. I wanted him there. I'd find him with his squared paper moving things around for the campus, making refinements, but not major changes. He always credited me with solving the problem of how to build on the mesa. My dorm, which is two levels up and two levels down, really wowed him, because he didn't think that way. So we got along fine.

The only time we didn't get along was when he suggested the Italian mosaic. I had never been to Europe. But he went whenever he could and had seen the small mosaics from Murano. "That's what we should use on these walls, Walter," he said.

"Oh," I said, "fine." So we got samples and I looked at them. Of course, we had a tradition of using red, blue, and yellow—the Bauhaus colors, which Gordon really stuck to. But I liked green also, so I brought along green. Gordon looked at me for a while and said, "Walter, if you use green I'll never go to another meeting." That was the easiest decision to make. I took off the green. I was raised at MIT, but he wasn't. I was sufficiently younger that I didn't have that full dedication to the Bauhaus that he had. He was really part of the revolution at the beginning, when America was modernizing. I was at the end of it.

DM: Did you run into any other problems on the Academy?

WN: The partners didn't like my chapel on the hill. It was too medieval. And Saarinen said, "I don't care what it looks like, but Walter, you've got to get it off that hill." He'd speak Finnish, you know. He was born in America, but would always go into a foreign language, and the words would come out marvelously. He used his hands and said, "Bring it down into the life of the cadets." Of course he was right, and it moved down, although very slowly. I often had a hard time because once we'd thought

something through, we thought that it didn't need to be reviewed again. There were times when it was proper to review, times when it was not. But Gordon would take the academic building, and he would suddenly start pushing elements around just for the sake of a Corbusian proportional system. I had a system too, based on the number seven. Three-and-a-half and seven. The whole Academy is based on the seven-foot module. I had lived in Japan and appreciated how the module of the tatami mat worked. But Americans are taller than they are, so I had to figure out a dimension that was appropriate. I picked three-and-a-half and seven. If you look at the Academy horizontally, vertically, within, everything is on that module ... Oh, it was a job to make it work rationally, but we did it.

DM: If you were accustomed to working with a rectangular module, how did you come to use the tetrahedron for the chapel?

WN: That was Ken Nasland's contribution, my engineer. We would have lunch at a beanery across the street and scribble while we talked. I was really worried because Gordon had sent me to Europe to look at Gothic architecture and Renaissance architecture. "Because you're going to do another con-troversial building, Walter, and you've got to be able to say that you've seen Chartres and Notre Dame." The trip took three weeks. I came back saying, "Gee, we don't have stone masons today. We don't have the love of labor through which something is added within the same vocabulary every decade. How can you achieve that effect, but do it all at once?" We made a little model of a folded plate, which was *au courant*. Take a piece of paper and bend it, and so forth. Origami. I started scribbling, drawing, trying to get a repetitive feature. Ken said, "What are you doing? Trying to draw a tetrahedron?" That's the way he talked. Very straight forward. I said, "No. What's a tetrahedron?" He drew me an *equal* tetrahedron. But I said that wouldn't work. "Well, make one of your own," he said. So I went home and got the tetrahedron to work. I worked as much at night as I did in the daytime. I got it to flip-flop. That was the great thing. I could flip-flop it, turn it upside down, inside out.

Then I made a model to show to Nat and Gordon. It was of two tetrahedrons and was about three feet tall. Of course Bruce Graham saw it in the office and asked, "What are you doing?" I said, "I'm working on the chapel." Nothing else happened. He went to Bill Hartman and said, "Walt is crazy. He's got an idea that's just awful." And then I took it to Nat who said, "Gee, that's wonderful." I took it to Gordon and he said, "You should pursue it." Bruce went to Gordon and said, "Will you stop it?" Gordon said, "No, I won't." So there was a conflict within the firm as well as outside the firm.

Our little studio was quite excited about it. We tried to make an apse, but nothing worked to our satisfaction, so we didn't do it. The idea grew of having three chapels in one. And I did traditional things like extend the shape of the stairway—a typical Renaissance trick. Then I did some studies on the glass in between. I waited for the Air Force to select an artist, but they told me they had no intention of selecting an artist, that I would have to do it. So I spent a year working with a team of four people who did research for me. Robinson Ward headed it. I said, "Robinson, how am I going to do all this glass? This mile of glass?"

DM: Were these people part of the studio?
WN: Yes.

DM: Dedicated to doing research?
WN: Yes, but I didn't get any approval. I just did it. Just four guys who concentrated on research—research on glass, research on aluminum, research on whatever was needed. As long as it was for the good of the project no one complained. The glass strips were only a foot in width, so I couldn't very well tell a story as Gothic stained glass had done. It had to simply work with colors. I went for dark colors at the beginning, symbolizing the creation of the world, shifting gradually to gold at the altar, for the revelation.

Robinson came up with the technique. He said, "Walter, you just take the workers and tell them to hit the edges with a hammer." The raised cushion would then fasten in different ways because the glass reacted differently to the way in which different people hit it. No one was trying to copy the old craft techniques of the Gothic cathedrals. "Just hit it. You've got a whole crate of them, hit them." And it worked. It *is* faceted and it looks great when the sunlight shines on it.

DM: It seems that, already then, you were able to achieve a fair bit of autonomy within the firm.
WN: Yes, and at the same time I was really in favor of working as a group. First of all, I had to concede that I could do it. Somehow I could do it. So I really wasn't worried about being in the group. That wasn't really a problem. Secondly, we were working on large projects, so there was an individual project within the group that you could take responsibility for. And then you had Nat. The partners' meetings were wonderful at that time. Gordon, of course, had established the name of the firm. All those project managers in New York, bless them—I mean, Fred Kraft, Ed Petrazzio, Bill Brown, and the rest of them—felt that Gordon took all the glory. No one got any credit in the magazines for any of the buildings until the Academy Chapel. Since half the partnership didn't want it built, they were very happy to let me take all the credit for designing it. So I broke a taboo by accident.

DM: Before we talk more about how you broke away from the mold within SOM, what would you say you took from the more orthodox modernist approach?
WN: I'm really the last contact from the old days at SOM. Bruce came after me by enough years that he caught the Mies bug, and John Barney Rogers, a partner in the firm in the beginning, went to school in the Bauhaus in Germany under Mies, spoke German. He was my boss when I was the designer out in the San Francisco office. I lived in a little one-room apartment with a view and a spring-down bed. When he went on vacation, he gave me the keys to his wonderful house in Pacific Heights, multileveled and looking out over Golden Gate Bridge. He had a library from Germany and chairs from Germany, tufted sofas and things. I'd take my vacation at the same time he did, and I'd go up there and see these elegant books. I was recently given an award at IIT, and I gave credit to Professor Anderson of MIT, to Gordon, and to John Barney Rogers. "Walter, this plan doesn't quite read," John would say because of his Miesian studies. It *reads*. You don't have to

look for it. A professional can immediately see how it works. So we all learned that part of modernism that has to do with reading. If you look at work by Le Corbusier or any of the other modernists, it always reads.

DM: Is that important to you still?
WN: Oh yes.

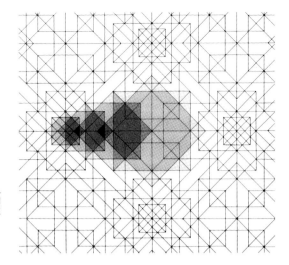

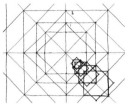
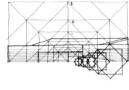

DM: Something you strive for in your work?
WN: Yes, even my complicated mathematical ones. I think you ought to have an image. In all my travels abroad I can't think of any place where chaos has been the design element. I've been to Bilbao like everybody else and seen the Guggenheim by Gehry. I think it's a marvelous building. I really do. But I can't imagine six of them.

DM: You've also described yourself in contrast to Mies who had a big influence on SOM. Would you say a bit more about that?
WN: I never could be a Mies fan. I just do not have the same basic attitude. The search for an SOM look was Nat's. Gordon was the closest to it at that time. I never thought of it to speak of. I didn't go home and think at night of being different. I'd go home at night and think, what are the issues I needed to deal with and why. Working on the campus at the University of Illinois I'd ask, "Why do I have a high-rise building? Because of the program?" We were trying to get the humanities and the social sciences to speak to one another. The president gave me the program. He didn't want all the departments in little buildings as they had at Urbana. So I devised a high-rise building that had two floors for each discipline with a seminar room in the middle and some offices. The elevators and the heating and

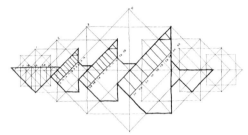

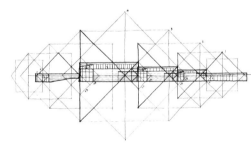

Field theory lattice studies, Miami University Art Museum, Oxford, Ohio ventilating system worked so that any two floors could operate independently on the weekend. We hoped there would be communication. We had a very modern, sixties attitude towards what an urban university should be. We thought it should provide skills and philosophies that would help resolve the urban problem. Of course it didn't. But the buildings reflected that effort.

DM: You start a project, then, by grappling with the task in its fullest sense. Then you look for the right architectural means to use, each time ending up with something quite different.
WN: Yes, but *that's* the MIT program. Professor Anderson was a marvelous man and a very Socratic critic. He would sit down by your drafting table and say, "Walter, why?" And you had to explain why you had done something. It was a Socratic world and a very good world. He was also a good modern architect. We could watch his swimming pool go up and know that we didn't have to copy him in any way. That was the way I was trained. I'm not a Mies man, you see. I'm an MIT man. We would do things differently at MIT. We would invent things.

DM: Can you talk a little bit about invention and experimentation?
WN: I just feel that technology is here for us to use and improve. It isn't a fixed subject.

DM: Is it true that mirrored glass was invented for the Air Force Academy?
WN: It was. You know, Jack Train, the engineer, and I invented the "finger" system for loading airplanes. Nat was a friend of the head of United Airlines. He asked me to solve the problem of Midway Airport: "How should we load an airplane?" So we did solve it. We had the ramp pull out for boarding and the luggage go on the moving carrier. Jack designed the moving carriages, but we didn't copyright them. They were used for the airport in Des Moines and at Midway Airport. Of course, things operated at a different scale then. You could drive up, drop your bag, and it would go on out on the finger. You didn't have the ticket office and so forth. So we've been inventive as a firm.

DM: You once said that you wanted to enhance the ability of the Air Force cadets to still be individuals in a context where they were being forced to be conformists.
WN: Right.

DM: Is this a recurring theme for you?
WN: It's my way of life: the individual in a group. I would become very unhappy sometimes. I'd come home and tell Dawn, "I've got to leave the firm. I'm just having too much trouble." And she'd say, "Walter, where are you going to get all that help from Sam Sachs? Where are you going to get the help from Ken Nasland," who was my engineer. So I learned. I found my clientele in higher education, which of course is not conservative. I was happy and developed my own studio. People would come to work with me because they knew of me. They would come to learn how to think. I didn't expect them to go out and become little "Netsches." When I used to hang all the work on the wall, the projects would seem very different from one another, which is more like Saarinen than Skidmore. In fact, that led to criticism from the partners. I didn't hold a line visually. Not like the box and variations on the box.

DM: You also didn't produce just a single alternative to the box.
WN: Well, I looked for one. That's what field theory was all about. I felt I had to make a contribution. I come from a town in which Sullivan made a contribution and Wright made a contribution. I should have to make a contribution too. Not that I was equal to them, but that was the role they played.

DM: Did your field theory develop from the chapel?
WN: It did.

DM: More than the rest of the Academy?
WN: Oh, yes. The Academy was straight out of MIT.

DM: How did geometry become so important to you?
WN: That came from my trip to Europe, whether it was a Greek temple or a Renaissance building or a Gothic building or an early medieval building.

DM: When you saw one of those buildings, did you see its geometry as if you had x-ray vision?
WN: Yes.

DM: How did you come to the word "field"? The designs you've been showing us are discrete objects, not field structures.
WN: Each one is a different field. There's a field of daisies, there's a field of sunflowers, there's a field of wheat.

DM: So you see each one of these as a field?
WN: Each one can be converted to a field.

DM: How would that conversion be made?
WN: It would depend on what the design is based on. You see how this geometry all connects, all these lines connect. This one is based on a theory of nine, the Hindu number. I grab a number like that. I'm Protestant, so I don't have a number.

DM: Why do you need numbers?
WN: We don't need numbers, I guess.

DM: Is the same thing true with geometry? How do you choose whether you'll start with a tetrahedron or a square or an octagon?
WN: The rotated square was the way we broke the box, by rotation.

DM: How did you go about make a drawing of that kind?
WN: Well, I tell you, Art and Architecture was the first building at UIC. It was a rotated square based around a circle. I made about a hundred drawings to explore that. We just drew them and drew them and drew them. The drawings weren't for any build-ing at all. They were just drawings.
This is an example of a field. This is a figure, a rotat-ing square is the figure of the field. They reduced in size mathematically, so that this one is equal to a half of the first, then a quarter, and this one. I bor-rowed the idea from a design by somebody in 2000 B.C. I didn't invent it. You see it makes a circle. You could use pieces of it. There's the whole one. And it's a very nice form to make changes with. It has change built into it. The rotated square is a fixed figure, while this is a floating figure. I used this a lot now, because I prefer the floating figure. Spaces float. Did you see my ginkgo leaf chair? You can sit on it and have a drink on one side and a book on the other. That's the idea.

DM: Why did you choose a ginkgo leaf?
WN: I did it just because of my excursion in Japan. I fell in love with a ginkgo tree. This is an apartment building that uses the same geometry. There it is and combined to make a field. Now this is where the figure has become a field.

DM: It's almost like a tissue.
WN: That's right. We flip-flopped the field and the figure. That forms the pattern as it goes up. We just exchanged that geometry for this geometry. You see? The big pieces and the little pieces.

DM: What's this one called?
WN: This is the chrysanthemum field, named after the flower of Japan, because I was doing a library for Sophia University using that and I wanted a word to communicate a love of Japan. It was the first time I did a linear core and the field went around the edge. The linear core was the book collection.

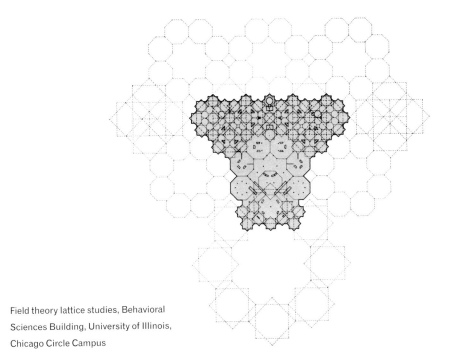

Field theory lattice studies, Behavioral
Sciences Building, University of Illinois,
Chicago Circle Campus

DM: Do you set up the geometry first and then somehow adapt it to the uses that the building is intended to for?
WN: No, I have that in the back of my mind as a goal. And I fiddle around until I get a geometry I know will work.

DM: Why do some of the projects have a very strong center while others don't?
WN: That comes from the program.

DM: How is the field theory different from working with a module?
WN: It uses a unit. A module is small scale and you repeat it. This is a field, a figure instead of a field. That's the figure out of the field. And this is a larger complex of figures that make a larger field.

DM: When it comes to turning the design into three dimensions, what do you think about?
WN: This is extruded, obviously. The whole chrysanthemum is working at the ground level, but then it disappears halfway in the roof. And then this other element intrudes.

DM: Your own house isn't an extrusion?
WN: No, it is not.

DM: It has so many shifting levels.
WN: Well, again, that comes from the program. I wanted to have one big space with no corners in the house. But I wanted to define the spaces. I could define them by levels—the living level, dining level, private bedroom level, with a little piece of the dining room coming into the living room.

DM: You respond to each individual situation.
WN: I'm just being like Wright. Because I do these variations within the scheme. I'm not interested in repeating anything if I can possibly avoid it. I can't claim Wright, of course. That would be conceited of me.

DM: How does your approach differ from Wright?
WN: I've looked at his plans since I was a kid. I went to the Robie House and the Blossom House. I can

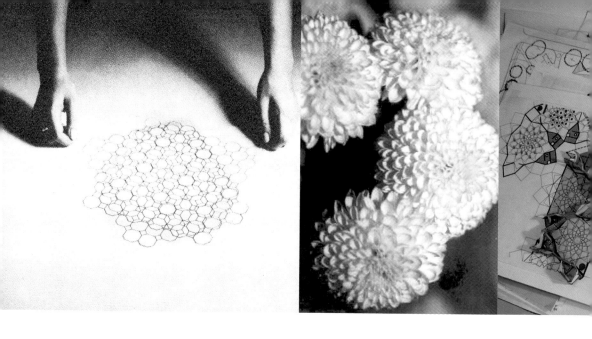

see the difference between the Blossom House and the Robie House.

DM: Sounds like you're thinking about variation.
WN: That's right.

DM: Is there a system involved at all?
WN: Unlike Gehry who has to do a different image each time, I am trying to work within the sense of figures and trying to develop a holistic relationship. That's all that I'm interested in doing. I didn't want to do another Air Force Academy. Never. It was fine. I did it. I worked like hell. It's a beautiful thing. It fits the setting. Fine.

DM: Some of your buildings remind me of Louis Kahn's work.
WN: Lou was part of my life. Lou and Bucky Fuller were two of my idols at the time.

DM: That's quite a combination.
WN: Yes, they are quite a combination. I knew Bucky from college. He'd give those three-hour, four- or five-hour lectures, and you had to sit there. We almost lost the Air Force Academy over Bucky. We didn't want to destroy the land by putting all the

little houses in. So we said, let's do a Bucky by lifting everything off the ground. We'd design a cluster, which gave us a small field where we didn't have to grade, we didn't have to touch anything. And we had a tower that cantilevered out letting you park under it and use it like a porch.
But the Air Force people just revolted. "You can have your modern Air Force Academy," they would say, "but I want my house to look just like it looked back home." So we almost got fired. They hired an architect from Omaha who did those kind of houses, and we worked with him to trim our houses up a little bit. But they had a flat roof. And we still tried to follow our site plan, but by the time they got through, the land was graded to hell. It was not what we wanted. To me that was a major loss in planning.
I was asked about a year ago to set criteria for an addition to the Academy. I said that people should work within the discipline of the Academy. Not copy it, but do something within the discipline. I thought that the chapel would be a good thing to deal with since there are now more religions that need to be all in the same building. I decided to work with the tetrahedron, to deconstruct it, and made many variations. This one is an imaginary tetrahedron on the

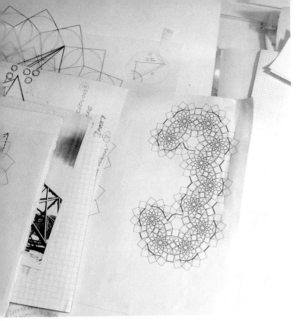

Housing units, Winnebago Children's Home, Neillsville, Wisconsin

DM: What about Gygory Kepes?
WN: Well, I didn't know Kepes. That was way after me.

DM: Kepes published a series of books that crossed over between science, technology, mathematics, art, and architecture. One was on structure, for instance.
WN: Oh, I've got the book.

DM: Another was on the module. What did you think of those when they came out?
WN: I know, I've got all these books. But some I like and some I don't. They're part of my language, you might say.

DM: Do any of the people you used to work with still work with field theory?
WN: No. It's too much hard work. I mean, you keep asking these questions. You have no idea what decision making involves. It's just hard work. I would sit there and do hundreds and hundreds of little patterns. Now I can do them on the computer, but before I used a compass and ruler, and then the copy machine.

DM: How did the technique of overlays work? What did that produce?
WN: Well, I was trying to break with the right angle. We did some studies on the rotated square in which they were not at right angles. Sixty degrees, thirty degrees. To see how that nested to make a field. Actually it did something very interesting. It left a void occasionally, which is of course chaos theory.

DM: Did you enjoy the way in which the field method could produce something unexpected?

outside. From the inside, it's scooped out, so you see it as an event. I made model after model after model. Then we had a show at John David Mooney Studio.

DM: You've taken geometries from the chrysanthemum and ginkgo leaves. Why do you look to nature as a source for design?
WN: Well, I'll tell you why. When I was a kid, my grandmother had a home in Lake Winnepesakee, a summer home, and we used to go up there. You wore no shoes and you got into the canoe and you went up and around. I was never an athlete. I guess if I had been an athlete I would be an entirely different person. So I collected leaves. I collected patterns and watched shadows. I wanted to be an artist. And my grandmother and I read; we read books. I became an intellectual early.

DM: Did you read D'Arcy Thompson?
WN: Oh, absolutely. I can't put my hand on it right now but it's here. Oh, yes. It was *On Growth and Form,* and it was given to me by Bob Engman at Penn, who knew it. He asked, "Walter, have you ever read *On Growth and Form*?" "No," I said, "I've just looked at it." So he gave me a copy.

WN: Oh yes. The studio would get all excited.

DM: What's the best building you've ever done?

WN: The library at Wells College. It's about to be torn down. I wanted to work with the environment, so I made it fit the site. In fact, the first design fit the site so well that I had to do the roof over again. I went to a meeting of trustees and was so excited when I explained that students could ski down the roof of this building. Afterward, the president said, "Walter, you better change the roof. The trustees were scared to death that the students will actually do that." So I changed the geometry, but it's still a very good building. It also fit the concept of what a library should be—a place where you study, put the book on the floor, and read on the floor or on pillows. It's not regimented. It has volume, it has space and perception. It has small rooms that you can go to, especially on the bridge. And it has native materials. It has brick and wood. So I felt it did all those things, plus. It's the first time we took three rotated squares and made them work together as a triad. The design of the library is different than any other field theory building because it's based on that triad.

DM: How did you get into collecting art?

WN: Gordon taught me to go to art galleries when we were working on the Air Force Academy. Gordon took me around to all the marvelous, very fancy galleries. He has a very fine collection, and he could afford it. He took me around, and the first thing he did was to march through the gallery and move gradually, very carefully—seeing what was on exhibit—into the back room. And he'd sit down, pull out his pipe, and say to the gallery director, who was there of course, "What's good today?" And they would haul out the Picassos, the Mirós and the Dubuffets, and the things that he liked. I would go around with him on Saturday after we had the meetings on the Academy. Later I would go on visual binges myself, after I got a bonus, and I'd spend twice what I had, hoping that another bonus would make up for it later.

DM: What was the first piece of art you ever bought?

WN: The first piece was a Motherwell.

DM: When you select a work, what do you look for?

WN: I don't look for field theory. I've been interested in Lichtenstein since we bought *Black Flowers* from his first show. I was in New York on one of my visual drunks, and the show was just coming down. It was the first benday dot painting that had been hand dyed. It was not mechanized. It was six hundred dollars. I bought it, took it home. I really loved it because of the contrast between the geometry of the background and the vase and the flowers. Kind of angry. Lichtenstein was a radical painter really. People don't realize it. They just think, "Oh, he does the funnies." That's not really true. I admire the way he works. The paintbrush. The Abstract Expressionists were hot, so he did brushstrokes that play on Abstract Expressionism. When Monet's *A Day In the Country* was traveling around, he did a series of takeoffs. Sometimes I buy a painting if I see a relation to the whole history of art, which I think is important, just like it is in architecture. Lichtenstein extends *A Day In the Country* to the modern style. I don't have to have a Monet, I have a Lichtenstein. It satisfies my desire. It's a good painting too.

DM: You said once that you thought that art works opened the mind. Can you say more about that?

WN: Well, I think I've been explaining that. I mean, there's a relationship between *A Day in the Country* and the whole of Impressionist painting. Here's a modern painter who does an Impressionist painter. I appreciate the fact that a modern artist today is not just denying the past. He's really doing the same thing I'm doing. He's working and exploring and expanding on Monet. Notice that the benday dots have disappeared. Now there are some stripes there.

DM: What should the firm be doing today that it might not be doing?

WN: Today it's as important to talk together as it was before, to establish a dialogue around real issues. Today's problem isn't breaking out of the box, it's blob theory. It's really three-dimensional geometry theory. It's tension theory. It's art theory. The Gehry art buildings. You can sit down and have a great session about these theories. How should they work within the firm? What do the partners think about them? What are the theories we want to project? It may not be one theory, but you may want to refine the different directions.

Now I don't know if the firm is doing blob theory. I could hardly get them to do a field theory building. Actually, I have some thoughts on field theory and the blob. How would I do a blob building in field theory? In a way, they flow into each other. The Moebius strip that has no beginning and no end. But Gordon and I would also talk about paintings. You can also develop the dialogue around art or music. I can list three, four, five composers from the 1950s and 1960s that I think are good. I like to play them with Chopin and go back to Ravel. Ravel is a traditionalist, but he did do some experimenting. So I'm interested in that.

Music and art were all a part of my life and I brought them into the studio. I feel that the profession is losing its relation to culture in general and to its own culture.

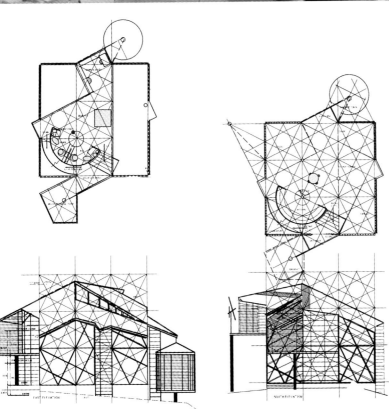

Project Credits

Renovation and Addition, Pennsylvania Station

CLIENT: Pennsylvania Station Redevelopment Corporation, United States Postal Service
DESIGN PARTNER: David M. Childs
PLANNING PARTNER: Marilyn J. Taylor
SENIOR DESIGNER: Ross Wimer
DESIGN TEAM: Anthony Pascocello, Michael Fei, Nazila Duran, Tran Vinh, Mi Yeon Kim, Scott Duncan, Carolyn Bemis, Ingo Jung, Vladimir Pajkic
SENIOR TECHNICAL COORDINATOR: Kevin Peters
TECHNICAL TEAM: Herbert Lynn, Raymond Hidalgo, Andrew Makin, Steven Danielpour, Carlos Infantes, Jennifer Chan, Christian Schreib, James VandeZande, Traci Nottingham, Michelle Lederer, Carlos Avila, Leeann Falciani, Alexis Garcia, Ivan Gartner, Clement Krug, Nikola Seferovic, Masha Dobrovolskaya
PROJECT MANAGER: Christopher McCready
STRUCTURAL AND MECHANICAL ENGINEERING: Ove Arup and Partners, Parsons Brinkerhoff Quade & Douglas
HISTORIC PRESERVATION ARCHITECT: Hardy Holzman Pfeiffer Associates

Training Facility, Kuwait Police College

CLIENT: Kuwait Ministry of the Interior
DESIGN PARTNER: Roger Duffy
STRUCTURAL DESIGN PARTNER: William Baker
MECHANICAL DESIGN PARTNER: Ray J. Clark
INTERIORS PARTNER: Stephen Apking
MANAGEMENT PARTNER: John Winkler
SENIOR DESIGNER: R. Anthony Fieldman
DESIGN TEAM: Scott Kirkham, Rebecca Behbahani, Brian Chung, Woong Yang, Andrew Liu, Nazila Shabestari, Neil Katz, Delis Papadapolous, Nurhan Gokturk, Jennifer Gannon, Taro Narahara, Philip Brown, John-Mark Capps, Diane Fischer, Peter Zaharatos
SPACE PLANNING: Robert Finger, Chul Moon, Carrie Ho, Christine Dzus
SENIOR TECHNICAL CO-ORDINATOR: Mark Igou
TECHNICAL TEAM: Angelo Arzano, Guy Punzi, Jon del Fierro, Mark Messina, Donald Marmen, Armando Gutierrez, Jeff Burke, Jaime Arroyuelo
PROJECT MANAGER: Imad Ghantous
STRUCTURAL ENGINEER: Ahmed Abdelrazaq
MECHANICAL ENGINEER: Joseph Jamal
ASSOCIATE ARCHITECTS: Gulf Consult

Office Building, 350 Madison Avenue

CLIENT: Max Capital Management Corporation
DESIGN PARTNER: Roger Duffy
MANAGEMENT PARTNER: John Winkler
SENIOR DESIGNER: Ross Wimer
PROJECT TEAM: Hilary Sample, Matt Williams, Scott Duncan, Malin Hedlund, Chul Moon, Chris Jensen, Sven Schroeter
TECHNICAL COORDINATOR: Jim Christerson
TECHNICAL TEAM: Tracy Nottingham, Chris Schreib, Ernesto Teran, George Verdadero
PROJECT MANAGER: Terry Dunn
STRUCTURAL ENGINEER: Gilsanz, Murray, Steficek, LLP
MECHANICAL ENGINEER: Sidney Barbanel
ELEVATOR CONSULTANT: Van Deusen & Associates

Bank Headquarters, Marina Bay

CLIENT: DBS Land
DESIGN PARTNER: David M. Childs, Mustafa Abadan
PLANNING PARTNER: Marilyn J. Taylor
STRUCTURAL DESIGN PARTNER: William Baker
SENIOR DESIGNER: Ross Wimer
DESIGN TEAM: Michael Fei, Ursula Schneider, Samer Bitar, Masha Dobrovolskaya, Kim Houston
PROJECT MANAGER: Hamid Kia
STRUCTURAL ENGINEER: Charles Besjak
STRUCTURAL DESIGN TEAM: Shane McCormick

Terminal Building, Changi International Airport

CLIENT: Civil Aviation Authority of Singapore
DESIGN PARTNER: David M. Childs
PLANNING PARTNER: Marilyn J. Taylor
STRUCTURAL DESIGN PARTNER: William Baker
SENIOR DESIGNER: Ross Wimer
DESIGN TEAM: Scott Duncan, Samer Bitar, Masha Dobrovolskaya, Michael Fei, So Young Kim, Ursula Schneider, Sven Schroeter, Tran Vinh, Sarah Dodson, Simone Pfeiffer
SENIOR TECHNICAL COORDINATOR: Mark Igou
TECHNICAL TEAM: Christopher Olsen, John McNulty, Perry Nunez, Jairo Arevalo
PROJECT MANAGER: Hamid Kia
STRUCTURAL ENGINEER: Charles Besjak
STRUCTURAL DESIGN TEAM: John Ashton, Barry Levin, Faiza Malik, Shane McCormick, Brian McEllhatten
ASSOCIATE ARCHITECT: PWD Consultants
LIGHTING CONSULTANT: Bartenbach Licht Labor

Case Studies: Glass and Steel Structural Systems

CLIENT: Canary Wharf Group, General Motors
DESIGN PARTNER: Adrian Smith
STRUCTURAL DESIGN PARTNER: William Baker
MANAGEMENT PARTNER: Jeffery McCarthy, Richard Tomlinson
SENIOR DESIGNER: Todd Halamka
PROJECT ENGINEER: Stan Korista
PROJECT MANAGER: Jonathan Orlove, Ed Thompson
Technical Coordinator: Anwar Hakim, Jason Stanley
PROJECT TEAM: J. T. Hsu, Kevin Klinger, Sierra Miester, Ryan Mullenix, Dane Rankin, Keith Sheehan, John Viise, Si Wu, Eric Zacherson
LIGHTING CONSULTANT: Bartenbach Licht Labor, Paul Marantz

Image Credits

Pennsylvania Station

K+D Lab: ill. 5
Jock Pottle/ESTO: ills. 7, 16, 17, 24, 34, 40, 41
Pixel by Pixel: ills. 9, 13, 18, 23, 42
Courtesy of United States Postal Service: ill. 11

Kuwait Police College

Advanced Media Design: ills. 10, 23, 32, 34

350 Madison Avenue

Jock Pottle/ESTO: ills. 6, 10, 15
Eduard Hueber: ills. 3, 14, 19, 21, 22, 23
dbox: ills. 18, 24

Marina Bay

Jock Pottle/ESTO: ills. 3, 4, 23, 25, 34, 37
K+D Lab: ill. 5
Advanced Media Design: ills. 22, 26, 30, 32

Changi Terminal Building

Pixel by Pixel: ills. 4, 8, 9, 10, 14
Roy Wright: ills. 6, 11, 12, 13
K+D Lab: ills. 40, 41

Walter Netsch Interview

Orlando R. Cabanban: ills. 10, 13
Balthazar Korab: ill. 5
Louis Reens: ills. 14, 15
Local History Collection: ills. 4, 5
Pikes Peak Library District
All other images provided courtesy of Walter Netsch

We have made every effort to find all copyright holders. However, should we have omitted to contact copyright holders in any individual instances, we would be most grateful if these copyright holders would inform us forthwith.

Edited by
Wilfried Wang

Copy editing
Tas Skorupa, Berlin

Design
COMA, Amsterdam/New York
with SOM

Reproduction
Franz Kaufmann GmbH,
Ostfildern-Ruit

Printed by
Dr. Cantz'sche Druckerei,
Ostfildern-Ruit

Published by
Hatje Cantz Verlag
Senefelderstraße 12
73760 Ostfildern-Ruit
Germany
Tel. +49/7 11/4 40 50
Fax +49/7 11/4 40 52 20
Internet: www.hatjecantz.de

DISTRIBUTION IN THE US
D.A.P., Distributed Art Publishers, Inc.
155 Avenue of the Americas,
Second Floor
New York, N.Y. 10013-1507 USA
Tel. +1 212-627 19 99
Fax +1 212-627 94 84

ISBN 3-7757-1089-2

Printed in Germany